Grace

Katy Warner

CURRENCY PRESS
The performing arts publisher

RED
STITCH | THE
ACTORS'
THEATRE

CURRENT THEATRE SERIES

First published in Australia 2022
by Currency Press Pty Ltd,
PO Box 2287, Strawberry Hills, NSW, 2012, Australia
enquiries@currency.com.au
www.currency.com.au

in association with Red Stitch Theatre, Melbourne.

Typeset by Integral for Currency Press.
Cover shows Mia Tuco, Kate Cole and Jillian Murray.
Cover image by Robert Blackburn. Cover design by Mathias Johansson.

Currency Press acknowledges the Traditional Owners of the Country on which
we live and work. We pay our respects to all Aboriginal and Torres Strait
Islander Elders, past and present.

Contents

Grace was first performed by Red Stitch Actors' Theatre at the Red Stitch Theatre, St Kilda, on 1 February 2022, with the following cast:

EMMA	Kate Cole
BETH	Jillian Murray
GRACE	Mia Tuco

Director and Production Dramaturg, Sarah Goodes
Set and Costume Design, Jacob Battista and Sophie Woodward
Lighting Design, Harrie Hogan
Music Composition and Sound Design, Grace Ferguson
Lighting Mentor, Paul Jackson
Dramaturg and Assistant Director, Ella Caldwell
Dramaturg, Tom Healey
Stage Manager, Natasha Marich
Assistant Stage Manager, Holly Anderson

This play was first developed through Red Stitch's INK writing program.

CHARACTERS

Emma	40s
Beth	Her mother, 60s–70s
Grace	Beth's granddaughter, 20s

SETTING

January 2020*

A suite in a 5-star hotel in Copenhagen. Winter.

*2020 was the warmest European winter on record (to date). Sadly, that January saw no snowfall in Copenhagen.

A NOTE ON THE TEXT

/   indicates the character with the next line of dialogue begins her speech

…   indicates the trailing off of a thought or idea

—   indicates a character is cut off mid-sentence

This play text went to press before the end of rehearsals and may differ from the play as performed.

SCENE ONE

Night. Copenhagen. A room in a hotel suite.

BETH *is chatting away as she enters the room with her daughter,* EMMA.

BETH: What do they speak here?

EMMA: Danish. You know that.

BETH: I couldn't understand a word / he said.

EMMA: He was speaking English.

BETH: Do all of them?

EMMA: A lot would, yes.

BETH: Okay. That—that makes me feel better.

EMMA: What?

BETH: It was all so last minute. If you'd given me more warning I could've learned a couple of words at least. That's polite, you know. To just attempt the language even if you're not very good at it. I like to at least make the effort.

EMMA: I gave you plenty of warning.

BETH: No—

EMMA: Months and months.

BETH: Fine. Whatever you say. I don't want to fight about it.

EMMA: No-one forced you to come.

BETH: What? You were going to come here all on your own?

EMMA: Yes.

BETH: You didn't have to bring me.

EMMA: I'm so sorry, Mum. I thought you'd love to see Europe.

BETH: Paris. I wanted to see Paris again. Not Europe.

EMMA: You do realise France is a part of Europe—

BETH: Paris is Paris. It's different. Entirely different.

EMMA: Whatever you say.

BETH: It's a very special place to me.

EMMA: I know.

BETH: Writing and drinking and smoking and fucking / all day long—

EMMA: Mum!

BETH: What?

EMMA: I don't want to hear it.

BETH: You're such a prude.

EMMA: No, I'm / not.

BETH: How did I raise such a prude?

EMMA: No idea.

BETH: [*taking in the room, finally*] This is nice. A little over the top but … nice …

EMMA: Yeah …

BETH: So?

EMMA: What?

BETH: Where do I sleep?

EMMA: Wherever you want.

BETH: I have my own room?

EMMA: Yes, Mum.

> BETH *goes to investigate the rest of the suite.*

BETH: [*off*] This is fancy.

EMMA: It is.

BETH: [*off*] I want this room.

EMMA: It's all yours.

BETH: [*off*] I need a wee!

EMMA: I'm sure there's a bathroom.

BETH: [*off*] There's two!

EMMA: Wow.

BETH: [*off*] I'm going to use this one.

EMMA: I don't need a running commentary, Mum.

BETH: [*off*] This is so fancy!

> EMMA *takes it all in—this incredible hotel, the fact that she is here in it, the extensive mini-bar and room service menu. A private moment of joy. She's finally 'made it'. Whatever that means …*

BETH: [*entering*] You sure I don't have to pay for any of this?

EMMA: I told you —

BETH: Because I couldn't.

EMMA: You won't have to, Mum.

BETH: You say that now but there could be a nasty surprise at the end of it all.

EMMA: There won't be.

BETH: You sure?

EMMA: It's all taken care of.

BETH: Hmm.

EMMA: What?

BETH: I didn't say anything.

EMMA: You made that noise.

BETH: No, I didn't.

EMMA: You did.

BETH: You're very lucky, you know.

EMMA: Lucky?

BETH: You are.

EMMA: Okay.

BETH: An award and a holiday—

EMMA: It's not really a holiday—

BETH: Very lucky.

EMMA: Fine.

BETH: No, you are. There are a lot of talented people out there who never get this sort of—what's the … this kind of … recognition. That's it. Recognition. We write and write, important things that actually mean something and we scrape by somehow and raise two children, two / children, Emma.

EMMA: I know, I know.

BETH: I just wonder what could have been. Sometimes. Nothing against you and your sister.

EMMA: No. Of course not.

BETH: I was a real writer.

EMMA: You still are.

BETH: Am I?

EMMA: You could write here. You might find some inspiration or something.

BETH: What? What would I write?

EMMA: I don't know. Whatever you want.

BETH: I'm tired.

EMMA: I didn't mean you had to start writing this very second.

BETH: I'm going to go to bed.

EMMA: Now?

BETH: I'm exhausted, aren't you / exhausted …

EMMA: I thought we could go for a walk and have a look around.

BETH: Don't be ridiculous; it's the middle of the night.

EMMA: It will help the jetlag.

BETH: But I'm tired.

EMMA: I know but it's better to walk first then sleep.

BETH: Who says?

EMMA: Everyone.

BETH: Doesn't sound right.

EMMA: It is.

BETH: Sounds like something you've made up.

EMMA: We're not here for long and I don't want us to miss any of it. We're in Copenhagen. Amazing, beautiful, Copenhagen.

BETH: You keep telling me that like I don't know.

EMMA: We should enjoy it.

BETH: I will. We will.

EMMA: If you go to sleep right now it's going to mess up your body clock—

BETH: We should have come earlier. I don't understand why we didn't come earlier.

EMMA: You've said.

BETH: We could have had a couple of days to adjust. It's a long way. Do they not understand that?

EMMA: I'm sure they understand.

BETH: Do they? I mean, they're all packed in so close together up here they forget about the other end of the world, don't they? Just completely forget about our very existence.

EMMA: They're giving me this award aren't they?

BETH: Took them long enough.

EMMA: Alright.

BETH: Could have done it a decade ago.

EMMA: They're doing it now.

BETH: A decade ago you were still writing at least. What do you do now?

EMMA: I write.

BETH: New things, Emma, when did you last write something new?

EMMA: I've just written that piece for The Guardian and—

BETH: Pft. The Guardian.

EMMA: You read The Guardian.

BETH: Books, Emma. Books, books, books. When did you last write a book?

EMMA: Didn't you want to go to bed?

BETH: I've got my second wind.

EMMA: Great—

BETH: Shit. Where are our bags?

EMMA: In the bedrooms.

BETH: Where are they?

EMMA: They put them in our rooms.

BETH: You can't take your eyes off them for a second—pickpockets and thieves, everywhere, they are, you need to be—to be—what's the …—alert, you need to be alert you can't trust—

During this EMMA *takes* BETH*'s hand and guides her to the bedroom door so she can see the bags for herself.*

EMMA: Mum. Mum. It's okay. Look, our bags are right here.

BETH: Who did that?

EMMA: The hotel staff.

BETH: Sneaky.

EMMA: It's their job, so—

BETH: You need to be careful. That's all. You can be a little too trusting sometimes and it's just going to get you into more trouble.

EMMA: Me?

BETH: Yes, you, you've always been too trusting, too ready to believe whatever anyone tells you.

EMMA: Doesn't sound like me.

BETH: You believed in unicorns for a very long time.

EMMA: You told me they were extinct. Like the dodo bird.

BETH: I was joking.

EMMA: I was five. I had no reason not to believe you.

BETH: But at fifteen?

EMMA: Okay.

BETH: It's very funny.

EMMA: It really isn't.

BETH: But then you changed.

EMMA: I grew up.

BETH: Stopped being my little free-spirited hippie.

EMMA: What are you talking about?

BETH: Got all serious and boring.

EMMA: Me?

BETH: You did.

EMMA: Okay.

BETH: I mean, look at this place. Once upon a time you never would have chosen a hotel like this.

EMMA: I didn't choose it.

BETH: Once upon a time you would have been shacking up in some dingy backpackers and telling me it was all part of the authentic experience.

EMMA: That doesn't sound like me.

BETH: Not anymore it doesn't.

EMMA: You want to stay in a shitty backpackers? Because I can arrange that for you. Right now.

BETH: I was reminiscing. That's all.

EMMA: Right, well, I'm going for a walk.

BETH: Thank you.

EMMA: What?

BETH: Don't know if I said it.

EMMA: Oh. Okay.

BETH: But I mean it.

EMMA: Well. You're—you're welcome.

BETH: I won't ruin all your fun.

EMMA: I didn't think you would.

BETH: Good. Because I won't.

EMMA: I invited you, Mum, remember?

BETH: Yes, I know, I know.

EMMA: I want you here.

BETH: That's very kind.

EMMA: It means a lot that you're here.

BETH: Well, it's—it's nice to be here.

EMMA: I mean it, Mum. I wanted us to have this. This moment. Together.

BETH: Watch out, you'll be telling me you love me in a minute.

EMMA: I do love you.

BETH: Might even give me a cuddle.

EMMA: A cuddle?

BETH: A hug. Now and then. It's not too much to ask for.

EMMA: I hug you.

BETH: When?

EMMA: I do.

BETH: Sophie would have loved this.

EMMA: Jesus. Okay. Yep.

BETH: Excuse me?

EMMA: Nothing, you were saying—

BETH: This is just very Sophie.

EMMA: Is it?

BETH: You should have asked her to join us.

EMMA: Well, I didn't.

BETH: She wouldn't have come but I think she would have liked to have been asked.

EMMA: I think she's fine.

BETH: You've spoken?

EMMA: No.

BETH: So how do you know?

EMMA: I wonder if they supply / toothpaste—

BETH: When did you last speak with her?

EMMA: Did you bring your own / toothpaste—

BETH: Emma?

EMMA: I can't remember.

BETH: I'm going to call her now, let her know we got in safe.

EMMA: Go for it.

BETH: Maybe you could say hello?

EMMA: Why?

BETH: Because it might be the last time you ever speak to her.

EMMA: What on earth are—

BETH: Terrorists, Emma—

EMMA: No, / Mum, honestly—

BETH: We could be mowed down by a terrorist and your poor sister would never get the chance to speak to you again.

EMMA: I'm going for a walk. You sure you don't want to come?

EMMA *goes to leave.*

BETH: Don't go.

EMMA: Mum!

BETH: You'll be lonely one day, Emma.

EMMA: I'm lonely now.

BETH: You're young so you don't think about it—

EMMA: I'm / not young—

BETH: You forget one day it will only be you, you and your books, and those books aren't going to be much company.

EMMA: Thanks for the tip.

BETH: No-one to call or visit or leave anything to.

EMMA: Stop it.

BETH: I'm not going to be around forever.

EMMA: And nor am I.

BETH: What is that supposed to mean?

EMMA: Nothing. It's …Go and call Sophie.

BETH: What's the time in Bali?

EMMA: Surprisingly, I have no idea.

BETH: Sophie's in Bali.

EMMA: I know. You've told me. Multiple times.

BETH: Family holiday. That's what she called it.

EMMA: Yes.

BETH: They didn't invite me.

EMMA: I know.

BETH: I'm family.

EMMA: But you got to come here instead.

BETH: Hmm.

EMMA: It's really lovely here. You'll love it.

BETH: It's very dark.

EMMA: Um, yeah, well, it's night, so…

BETH: I know, I know, but it feels darker, doesn't it? Like a deeper sort of dark.

EMMA: Okay.

BETH: Inky.

EMMA: What?

BETH: The sky. The sky is inky. Don't you think?

EMMA: Yeah, yeah it is.

BETH: I'll just send a text message. Let her know we got in okay. She'll be worried she hasn't heard, you know what she's like.

EMMA: Whatever you want, Mum.

BETH: And we can go for a stroll in the morning.

EMMA: I'm going to go for a quick one now but once you're up—

BETH: No, no you need to stay here, just stay here, please.

EMMA: I'm just going to go around the block, stretch my legs.
BETH: But what if I wake up before you're back?
EMMA: What about it?
BETH: What will I do?
EMMA: I don't know. Have a bath, read a book, watch television—
BETH: Could you just stay?
EMMA: I want to stretch my legs a bit.
BETH: This room is huge. You could stretch your legs right here.
EMMA: We're in Copenhagen, Mum—we should actually see the place.
BETH: And we will, just not right now. I'm tired.
EMMA: But—
BETH: Please stay.
EMMA: Mum.
BETH: It's late. You could get mugged.
EMMA: I don't think people get mugged in Copenhagen.
BETH: How do you know?
EMMA: I just know.
BETH: I—I'd like you to be here. I'd feel better. If you were here.
EMMA: You're perfectly safe.
BETH: It's just so dark out. You shouldn't wander around a strange city in the dark. Please. Don't. I'll worry.
EMMA: Alright.
BETH: Promise?
EMMA: Yes. I'll be right here.
BETH: Don't say it like that.
EMMA: Like what?
BETH: Like it's a chore.
EMMA: I didn't—
BETH: Look at your face.
EMMA :It's fine. I'll wait here.
BETH: [*as she exits*] Bonne nuit ma fille.
EMMA :We're not in Paris, Mum.
BETH: [*off*] Don't remind me.
EMMA: [*under her breath*] Oh my god …

> EMMA *relaxes. Maybe she kicks off her shoes, if she hasn't already, takes a small bottle of champagne and a glass from the mini bar and wanders off stage to her bedroom.*

The room relaxes.

A mobile phone rings from Emma's room. She answers the phone offstage.

EMMA: [*off*] Hi Penny! It's so good to—... What? ... Wait—wait a second ... No, I can't—... Because I don't want to ... Fucking hell ... No, no, fine ... I get it ... Okay ... Yep ... Bye then.

EMMA *shouts in frustration. Storms from her room, carrying her laptop and headphones, muttering and swearing.*

BETH *enters.*

BETH: What's going on?

EMMA: Go back to bed.

BETH: Is something the matter?

EMMA: Everything's fine.

BETH: Why are you wearing that?

EMMA: Sorry?

BETH: That—that robe.

EMMA: Um, I—

BETH: You look ridiculous.

EMMA: I was going to have a bath.

BETH: In that?

EMMA: Anyway, I can't now.

BETH: Why not?

EMMA: I've got to do this fucking interview.

BETH: Now?

EMMA: Yep.

BETH: Wearing that?

EMMA: [*as she exits, continuing the conversation from her room*] I'm getting changed, obviously.

BETH: Where's this happening then?

EMMA: [*off*] Online.

BETH: Where?

EMMA: [*off*] They're calling me.

BETH: *Calling* you? Who's calling you?

EMMA: [*off*] One of those TV breakfast shows, back home.

BETH: Good god.

EMMA: [*off*] What?

BETH: They're doing it now?

>*Beat*

Can you hear me?

>EMMA *enters, now dressed in a mish-mash of clothing. As they speak,* EMMA *quickly sets up the laptop for the Skype interview.*

EMMA: You have to be quiet or go to bed.

BETH: Charming.

EMMA: They're going to Skype me / in now—

BETH: They're what?

EMMA: Skyping?

BETH: What for?

EMMA: The interview. They're doing it online.

BETH: Sounds horrendous.

EMMA: Yeah, / well—

BETH: And they're doing that right now?

EMMA: That's what I said, Mum.

BETH: But you're so—I mean, you're very—you're flustered.

EMMA: Yes.

BETH: Ask them to reschedule.

EMMA: I can't.

BETH: You have to do it here?

EMMA: Where else am I going to do it?

BETH: Surely they could—I mean would it kill them to get you in a studio, with lights and makeup—the lighting in here is awful, you'll look awful—

EMMA: Thanks, Mum.

BETH: Why don't they send a camera crew? They do that sort of thing, surely?

EMMA: Not for me they don't.

BETH: But the award—

EMMA: I'm lucky to be getting this interview.

BETH: Hmm.

EMMA: Penny only got the call because someone dropped out on them. Last minute.

BETH: I bet it was a footballer.

EMMA: What?

BETH: Who dropped out.

EMMA: I don't know.

BETH: I do. Whole bloody country is obsessed with stupid, mind-numbing sport. Sport! Turn our noses up at anything remotely intellectual, anything remotely literary, anything that holds any kind of significance beyond a football oval.

EMMA: Not now, Mum.

BETH: They should be celebrating you like they do those knuckle-head / footballers—

EMMA: Knuckle-heads?

BETH: They should be paying you those million-dollar contracts.

EMMA: Shush.

BETH: You need some blush.

EMMA: I don't have time.

BETH: For God's sake, Emma, you're going to be on national television, you can make time for a bit of blush. And lipstick.

EMMA: Mum!

> BETH *rushes off to get her make-up bag.*

BETH: [*off*] It won't take a second.

EMMA: Leave it. It doesn't matter.

BETH: [*off*] Of course it matters.

> EMMA *puts the finishing touches to her laptop set up, plugs in the headphones and puts them on, as* BETH *returns—armed with blush, brush, lipstick. She lunges towards* EMMA.

EMMA: [*whispering*] No, no—

BETH: You look like a corpse.

EMMA: Fuck, Mum, stop—

BETH: I'm trying to help

EMMA: [*to the screen*] Hello … Yes, I can hear—… Right … okay … yes, yes, got it …

> *Silence*

BETH: [*whispering*] What's happening?

> EMMA *gestures to her mother to be quiet.*

EMMA: [*to an unseen producer on the screen*] Thank you for having me, I'm a big fan of the show … Yes, I'm in Copenhagen right now … It's pretty late here … Oh, no, no problem at all … I'm so thrilled, really, thrilled, by the recognition, it means a lot … Yeah, it's for my body of work so you probably know *Ruby The Forgotten Mouse*—… Yep … that's it—that's the one … Oh, that's really lovely of you to say … But this is for all of them … Twelve … Yes, it's a lot I suppose … It's an international award—they actually call it The Little Nobel Prize which is kinda sweet really [*forced laughter*] … Oh no, no, I'm still writing, no, no, not dead, I'm here, I'm writing, I haven't died [*that forced laughter again*] you can't get rid of me that easily! … Ohh, no, it's not writer's block it's just the way it goes. You know? Um. It can just take time. Writing of any kind can take time … It's been about ten years … Yes, yes, I know they still read them and they're still in print so it feels like I'm still—… A decade since—… Yep, a long time between—… Yeah … Well, I'll tell you first there are talks about turning Ruby into an animated film which is very exciting and—… I'm very excited … I can't say too much, there's still a lot of, um, discussion, you know, to be had but I um, I hope that it might help bring the stories to life for a whole new generation—… I think it will be very special. Something for families, to share, you know, bond over and—… Right, yes, well thank you for having me. Thank—

She's cut off.

Silence. She removes her headphones. Closes the lid of the laptop.

BETH: That was it?

EMMA: Seems like it.

BETH: Was it that blonde one?

EMMA: Sorry?

BETH: Interviewing you? The chirpy blonde one?

EMMA: Maybe.

BETH: Hate that one.

EMMA: Good to know.

BETH: So irritating. The voice. And that laugh. Ugh. Grates on me.

EMMA*'s mobile rings.*

BETH: You want me to— .

EMMA: Leave it.

BETH: But—

The phone stops ringing. EMMA *turns off her phone.*

BETH: You told them about the movie.

EMMA: I know.

BETH: Oopsy.

EMMA: I got flustered.

BETH: I could tell.

EMMA: I had to give them something.

BETH: At least you didn't say the D-word.

EMMA: Penny's going to kill me.

BETH: Screw Penny.

EMMA: She's worked really hard for this—all this negotiating and ego stroking—

BETH: That's her job, isn't it?

EMMA: And then I go and open my big fucking mouth on national television—

BETH: I don't think many people watch it to be honest.

EMMA: I told her not to let me do interviews.

BETH: You sabotage yourself, Emma. That's what you do.

EMMA: I just get nervous. That's all. Tongue tied and stupid and I fucking hate fucking interviews.

BETH: You're just not very good at them.

EMMA: Yes. I know that.

BETH: And look, the truth of the matter is, you've always hated Disney.

EMMA: What? Why would you—what are you talking about?

BETH: You did it on purpose because you don't really want to work with them. You hate Disney.

EMMA: Stop saying that. I don't hate Disney—what kind of arsehole hates Disney?

BETH: You.

EMMA: That's not true. And please don't keep saying that. Okay? Please don't say that.

BETH: You said it yourself.

EMMA: When?

BETH: *The Little Mermaid.*

EMMA: Oh.

BETH: Aha.

EMMA: Okay.

BETH: See?

EMMA: That's different.

BETH: You have told many, many people, many, many times that *The Little Mermaid* is diabolic.

EMMA: I didn't.

BETH: You get very mouthy about it.

EMMA: Mouthy?

BETH: Do they know?

EMMA: Know what?

BETH: Your feeling towards *The Little Mermaid*.

EMMA: Weirdly it's never come up.

BETH: It will though.

EMMA: No it / won't.

BETH: They'll find out.

EMMA: How on earth—

BETH: You would have ranted about it to the wrong person, you wait, you'll see—

EMMA: I don't rant.

BETH: You get very ranty up on that high horse of yours and you forget, you forget they're always listening.

EMMA: Who?

BETH: Everyone.

EMMA: Alright.

BETH: When are you meeting them?

EMMA: Tomorrow, I think—oh my god, I've screwed it all up. I have. I can't believe I did that.

BETH: Don't take it so seriously.

EMMA: It is serious. It's my work.

BETH: It'll be fine.

EMMA: It won't. I'm awful at this stuff.

BETH: You're a writer not a public speaker.

EMMA: Thanks a lot, Mum.

BETH: In the morning everything will seem so much better.

EMMA: You always say that.

BETH: Because it's true.

EMMA: I'm going for a walk.

BETH: Emma. Please. I've asked you—

EMMA: I need to get out of here. You'll be fine.

BETH: Emma.

EMMA: I'll be quick. Fifteen minutes. I just—I have to, sorry, I can't—

BETH: Stop being so hard on yourself.

EMMA: I'll be back soon.

> *She goes to leave.*

BETH: Wait, wait, I'll come with you.

EMMA: You will?

BETH: Yes. Of course. I'll just—I need my coat.

EMMA: Get it then.

BETH: Don't leave without me.

EMMA: I wouldn't …

> BETH *exits.*

> EMMA *takes a moment to compose herself. A deep breath. A forcing back of the ridiculous tears she really doesn't want to shed right now. Or ever. It was only an interview.*

BETH: [*entering*] Okay?

EMMA: Okay.

> *They exit. Together.*

SCENE TWO

Very early the following morning. Dark.

BETH *wanders into the room. She is here but not really here. Half sleeping, half waking. She is dancing, a shuffled, muted version of a waltz. The version in her mind is probably much grander. She speaks to someone who isn't there.*

BETH: Hopeless … just … I've tried—tried many, many things … hopeless … hopeless… don't stop dancing … keep dancing … dancing … feet … you think you're so clever …

> *A light turns on. It's* EMMA, *entering from her bedroom.* BETH *stops.*

EMMA: Mum?

BETH: —

EMMA: Mum? What are you doing?

BETH: Is she here?

EMMA: What?

BETH: She should be here. Should be here by now.

EMMA: Who?

BETH: —

EMMA: Mum?

BETH: Never mind, never mind—

EMMA: What are you doing out here?

BETH: I don't know …

EMMA: It's the middle of the night.

BETH: I know—I know that.

EMMA: You alright?

BETH: Fine.

EMMA: Sleepwalking?

BETH: No ... I … I …

EMMA: Mum …

BETH: I want a glass of water.

EMMA: Okay.

BETH: I only came out for a glass of water.

EMMA: Okay.

> *Silence as* EMMA *retrieves a bottle of water from the mini bar.* BETH *looks out the window.* EMMA *opens the bottle of water before handing it to her mother.*

BETH: There's nobody out there.

EMMA: It's very early.

BETH: No-one at all.

EMMA: No.

BETH: I don't like that. There should be people out there. Where are they, you think?

EMMA: Asleep.

BETH: No, no, no, those streets out there need people—there should be people out there. Something's wrong.

EMMA: Nothing's wrong, Mum.

BETH: Are you sure?

EMMA: I'm sure.

> *Silence.*

BETH: Thank you for making me go out there. For a walk.

EMMA: I didn't make you.

BETH: It was nice.

EMMA: It was supposed to help you sleep.

BETH: Sorry.

EMMA: What for?

BETH: Waking you.

EMMA: I was awake.

BETH: Do you think it will snow?

EMMA: Maybe …

BETH: Strange, isn't it? We've gone from fire to snow. Just like that.

EMMA: We're on the other side of the world, Mum.

BETH: I know, but still, it's something, isn't it?

EMMA: I suppose.

BETH: I hope it snows.

EMMA: White bees.

BETH: What are you talking about?

EMMA: The old lady tells her grandson that the snowflakes are white bees swarming, and their queen is the snow queen. You remember that one?

BETH: Ah, yes, I think so …

EMMA: He is taken by the Snow Queen and the little girl goes on that journey to save him.

BETH: She was his sister.

EMMA: No, she wasn't. They were friends.

BETH: I remember it differently.

EMMA: Of course you do.

BETH: What does that mean?

EMMA: He has glass caught in his eyes and his heart. Which meant he could only see the ugliness and meanness of the world. And so he turned cold and heartless. And when the little girl found him, it was her warm tears which dislodged the glass and helped him see the beauty of world again.

BETH: Do you know, your gran never saw snow.

EMMA: Didn't she?

BETH: I think that's very sad.

EMMA: Maybe she didn't want to. Maybe she was happy with the things she was able to see.

BETH: She was never happy.
EMMA: No. You're right.
BETH: I never wanted to be like her.
EMMA: You're not.
BETH: Good.

> *They look out the window.*

We should leave a light on.
EMMA: Alright.
BETH: It's awfully dark. I don't like it.
EMMA: We can keep this lamp on. How about that?
BETH: Good, good.
EMMA: You should go back to bed.
BETH: I might wait … Just a moment.

> BETH *sits on the couch.*

EMMA: We really need to try and sleep.
BETH: Just come, sit, with me, for a moment.
EMMA: Mum.
BETH: Sit.

> EMMA *sits on the couch next to her mother.*

EMMA: Now what?
BETH: Nothing.

> *They sit in silence.*

> EMMA *eventually lays her head in her mother's lap.*

SCENE THREE

Next morning. A more respectable hour for waking up. And yet … no-one is awake.

A knock at the door.

Nothing.

The ring of the doorbell.

EMMA *emerges, still not fully awake, and makes her way to the front door. As she opens it a young woman pushes through into the room, drops her bag onto the floor, flustered, desperate … she's about to throw up. This is* GRACE *but* EMMA *doesn't know that … yet …*

GRACE: Bathroom? Bathroom?

EMMA: Um, that way, just through there—

> GRACE *rushes offstage.* EMMA *picks up her bag and waits—unsure whether to go in there.*

EMMA: [*towards the bathroom*] Hello? You alright?

GRACE: [*returning to the room*] False alarm.

EMMA: Oh.

GRACE: Sorry, sorry about that.

EMMA: You alright?

GRACE: Oh my god, sorry, I'm so embarrassed.

EMMA: Don't be.

GRACE: Sorry.

EMMA: You want some water or—

GRACE: Thanks. Sorry. Yes, thanks.

EMMA: Here's your bag—

GRACE: Oh, thanks, sorry—

EMMA: [*getting* GRACE *water*] That's a lot of sorrys.

GRACE: Yeah, well …

EMMA: Water. Drink.

> GRACE *does.*

GRACE: Thanks. Motion sickness, you know? Do you get that, too? From the drive. It sort of just builds up and then, wham, you know? It's embarrassing. I'm so sorry.

EMMA: So, um, this is 506.

GRACE: What?

EMMA: Room 506. Where are you meant to be?

GRACE: Emma.

EMMA: Um, sorry—

GRACE: Emma, it's me.

> *Pause*

EMMA: Grace?

GRACE: Hi.

EMMA: God. I …

GRACE: Surprise.

EMMA: Oh …

GRACE: Not the entrance I'd planned.

EMMA: Oh, yeah, no, that was—you feeling alright now?

GRACE: I might just sit for a—

EMMA: Oh, god, of course, sit, sit, you need more water or—

GRACE: I'll be okay.

EMMA: Motion sickness?

GRACE: Yeah.

EMMA: Ginger.

GRACE: What?

EMMA: Ginger helps with that. I think.

GRACE: Oh.

EMMA: I can get you some, we might have some / ginger beer actually or—

GRACE: No, no, no, please, don't—don't worry.

Silence

EMMA: Wow. It's you.

GRACE: It's me.

EMMA: You're here. In Copenhagen.

GRACE: Yep.

EMMA: Um, why?

GRACE: Oh—um—I—I just—I … I read about the award and I knew you were gonna be here and it seemed like a good idea to, you know, come say hi and—

EMMA: Look, if you'd called ahead and let me know we could have worked something out but—

GRACE: Oh my god. Sorry. I've stuffed up. Sorry.

EMMA: No, it's just a shock. That's all. I didn't—wasn't—wasn't expecting you—

GRACE: You didn't recognize me.

EMMA: No. I didn't.

GRACE: I look a bit different now.

EMMA: A bit. Yes.

GRACE: This is a nice room.

EMMA: Yes.

GRACE: This is my first time in Copenhagen.

Beat.

In the taxi, on the way from the airport, I was just staring out the window like, like wow, you know, wow, it's looks like a movie-set or something, it doesn't seem real.

Pause

EMMA: I have to get ready for this thing—

GRACE: The lecture.

EMMA: Yes. That's it. That's … Sorry, did you—it's a long way to come, Grace.

GRACE: Not really. I live in London.

EMMA: London?

GRACE: Manchester, actually, but London sounds better. Didn't you know?

EMMA: Yeah, I think—it sounds familiar.

GRACE: It's been a year. Almost. Teaching there. Or trying to cos they don't really listen to me so it's not like I'm really teaching them anything, it's kinda more like crowd control and I'm not even so good at that … yeah … But it's an experience, so …

EMMA: Good for you.

GRACE: Yeah, it's—it's good. I like it. I mean I'm living in this share-house which is a bit gross but the guys I live with are nice and I'm travelling a lot and—

EMMA: Sorry, Grace, I can't—I have to get ready, I have a lot on today.

GRACE: I thought I could come.

EMMA: Where?

GRACE: To the lecture.

EMMA: No.

GRACE: And the ceremony, maybe—

EMMA: That's not how it works.

GRACE: Of course. No. Sorry. I should have spoken with you first, but we thought it would be a nice surprise, you know: Surprise! Because I haven't seen you for ages and this is really special, all of this, and I wanted to see you and cheer you on and I thought you'd be happy and …

EMMA: I really don't need cheering on.

Pause

You feeling any better?

GRACE: Yeah, thanks.

EMMA: Are you hungry?

GRACE: Um.

EMMA: I'm starving. You want some breakfast?

GRACE: Is that okay?

EMMA: I wouldn't have asked if it wasn't.

GRACE: Um, I don't wanna get in the way.

EMMA: Food. Would you like some food?

GRACE: Sure.

EMMA: You still like scrambled eggs?

GRACE: Sounds good.

EMMA: Done. I'll just—

GRACE: Can I stay?

Pause

EMMA: Let me order breakfast.

EMMA *exits.*

GRACE *lays down on the floor, closes her eyes, breathes.*

BETH *enters.*

GRACE: Nan!

BETH: You're late.

GRACE: No, I'm not.

BETH: You sure?

GRACE: It didn't work.

BETH: What didn't?

GRACE: Emma. She's not happy-surprised, she's angry-surprised.

BETH: No, she isn't.

GRACE: You didn't see her face.

BETH: Never mind that—did you know we flew business class. Hey? How about that? Business. Class.

GRACE: Nan—

BETH: It was very fancy. We had our / own—

GRACE: I told you we should have warned her, mentioned it, you know?

BETH: She would have said no. You know what she's like.

GRACE: Do I?

BETH: I know her and she would have said no.

GRACE: Nan! You knew she was going to be pissed. Why did you let me
do that?

BETH: You know that saying.

GRACE: What saying?

BETH: You know the one—better to seek forgiveness than ask permission,
or something like that.

GRACE: Geez, Nan.

BETH: Well, you're here now and I assume you're staying, yes? She said
you could stay?

GRACE: She's ordering us breakfast.

BETH: That sounds like a good sign.

GRACE: You think?

BETH: Yes! … So, you going to give me a hug, say hello, all that?

GRACE: Sorry.

BETH: Come here then.

> GRACE *does. She hugs her grandmother.*

You've lost weight.

GRACE: Um, I don't—no, don't think so.

BETH: You happy?

GRACE: Yeah, sure.

BETH: Any news?

GRACE: Not really.

BETH: I'm starving. Hope she's ordering me breakfast.

GRACE: I can check.

BETH: No, no, don't bother, I'll go, I'll go—

EMMA: [*as she enters*] Food is on its way.

BETH: For me?

EMMA: Yes.

BETH: I'd like an omelette. Did you order me an omelette?

EMMA: Scrambled eggs.

BETH: I wanted an omelette.

EMMA: Same thing.

BETH: No / it's not.

EMMA: We have a visitor.

BETH: I see.

GRACE: Nan actually / told me that—

BETH: I think she should stay with us.

EMMA: Oh, I, um—

BETH: There's plenty of room. It will be nice. Spending time together.

GRACE: Thanks, Nan.

EMMA: I'm going to be very busy.

GRACE: I know. The award. It's amazing … No, no, I meant, I didn't mean—not amazing like *I can't believe it* because of course I can believe it, I do believe it, you're totally deserving and just … The award. It's. Amazing. You know?

BETH: She knows.

EMMA: Awards are a bit ridiculous, aren't they?

GRACE: Yeah, yeah, of course.

BETH: Until you get one.

EMMA: Mum.

BETH: Admit it. You're bloody excited and so you should be. It's a big deal. And we're all here to celebrate.

EMMA: It's not bad.

BETH: Not bad? You know what they call it, this award she's getting, you know the nickname they give it?

GRACE: Um, no I—

BETH: The Little Nobel Prize.

GRACE: Wow.

BETH: It's not actually a Nobel Prize.

GRACE: Oh, no, no, I know.

BETH: But that's what they call it. The Hans Christian Andersen award. A Little Nobel Prize.

EMMA: Alright, Mum, I'm sure Grace doesn't need to hear all of this. [*To* GRACE] You'll have to sleep on the sofa.

GRACE: That's fine, that's better / than fine, that's —

EMMA: Alright.

GRACE: Thank you.

EMMA: Alright.

GRACE: You won't even know I'm here.

BETH: You should go have a shower, freshen up a bit.

GRACE: Um, okay, you sure?

BETH: You look like one of those, those backpackers.

GRACE: Oh, yeah, right.

BETH: We flew business class.

GRACE: You've said.

EMMA: She can't let it go.

BETH: There's two bathrooms.

GRACE: Wow.

BETH: They're through there.

GRACE: Right. Cool. Thanks. Again. For, um, yeah …

GRACE *exits.*

EMMA: Did you know about this?

BETH: Nope.

EMMA: You're such a liar.

BETH: She's not hurting anyone by being here, is she?

EMMA: I really don't have time for this.

BETH: And I really wish you'd ordered me an omelette.

EMMA: There's a whole city out there, Mum, full of all the omelettes you could ever desire—you can always go and get one.

BETH: On my own?

EMMA: Call room service and change the order then.

BETH: I'll cope, I'll cope.

EMMA: She waltzes in here, like it's this great surprise—very immature, really, immature and—and—impulsive.

BETH: Hmm.

EMMA: You had something to do with this, didn't you? Mum?

BETH: —

EMMA: Mum?

BETH: You can't just cut people out of your life like that, no matter how hard you try.

EMMA: For god's sake. I didn't cut her out.

BETH: What would you call it?

EMMA: I'm not getting into this now.

BETH: She's not hurting anyone.

EMMA: I had plans.

BETH: Oh well.

EMMA: Oh well? This was supposed to be—I mean, I wanted to share it with you, Mum—

BETH: You are sharing it with me. I'm right here.

EMMA: I know I keep saying it's not a big deal but, it is, and I had a picture in my mind of how it would go and—and this was meant to be something for you and me, Mum. You and me.

BETH: You haven't seen her in years, Emma. Years.

EMMA: So why now? Why not next week? Next month? Maybe I can go visit her after all this. Let's do that. We can arrange that, can't we? That wouldn't be hard.

BETH: She's here now.

EMMA: Can you send her home?

BETH: No, I will not.

EMMA: Please?

BETH: For god's sake, I will not do that to the poor child.

EMMA: She isn't a child.

BETH: And neither are you.

EMMA: I don't want her here.

BETH: That's an awful thing to say.

EMMA: I'm not going to say it to her, am I. God, Mum, I'm not a monster.

BETH: She's staying, and you're just going to have to deal with it.

> GRACE, *enters. It isn't entirely clear to* EMMA *or* BETH *if she has overheard them. But she has. Of course.*

GRACE: That shower is amazing.

BETH: Did you actually shower?

GRACE: Yes.

BETH: You were very quick.

GRACE: I didn't want to hold anyone up.

BETH: Did you wash?

GRACE: Nan. Yes. Of course. God.

BETH: Hmm.

GRACE: I did!

BETH: Whatever you say.

EMMA: Right. Well. I need to get ready—

BETH: What time is this lecture?

EMMA: It doesn't matter because you're not coming.

BETH: Since when?

EMMA: Since our visitor showed up.

GRACE: Oh, I—I have tickets.

EMMA: What?

GRACE: I bought tickets. For the lecture.
BETH: How about that?
GRACE: It sounds great.
EMMA: You'll be bored.
GRACE: No, I won't.
BETH: Can I come, too?
GRACE: I got two.
BETH: How about that?
EMMA: Happy?
BETH: Yes.
EMMA: I'm having a bath.
BETH: Alright, alright.

EMMA *exits.*

GRACE: Did I do something wrong?
BETH: We both did. Don't worry about it.
GRACE: I thought—
BETH: Come here.
GRACE: Why?
BETH: Your hair, you look homeless—
GRACE: You shouldn't say that.
BETH: Let me brush it.
GRACE: I'm not a kid anymore.
BETH: Come on, let me.
GRACE: Geez.
BETH: Come on, bring your brush.

GRACE *takes a brush from her bag and sits in front of her grandmother, who proceeds to brush her hair.*

GRACE: I shouldn't have come.
BETH: Well, you're here now.
GRACE: Ow, be gentle.
BETH: So many knots.
GRACE: I know, I know.

Silence

BETH: Missed you at Christmas.
GRACE: I know.

BETH: You could have called.
GRACE: I did.
BETH: Did you?
GRACE: Yeah.
BETH: So, what's new?
GRACE: Nothing.
BETH: Boyfriend?
GRACE: No.
BETH: Girlfriend?
GRACE: No.
BETH: Sex?
GRACE: Nan.
BETH: What?
GRACE: I'm not talking to you about this.

> *Silence.* BETH *brushes* GRACE'*s hair.*

BETH: You want bunches?
GRACE: What?
BETH: Like this?

> *She pulls* GRACES'*s hair into piggy tails.*

GRACE: No way!
BETH: I used to wear my hair like that. My mother called them bunches. We call them piggy tails.
GRACE: No, thanks.
BETH: There's a moment and I don't know if I remember—if I remember it as it happened, or if I remember it because of the photograph. My hair is in bunches—up, like that … I remember it was hurting my scalp because she always … you see, Mum didn't like it to fall out during the day but it always would, even when she parted it so tight down the middle … it hurt. But maybe this … this might've been a different time and I'm just transposing it onto this. Maybe … Anyway, I'm wearing a red polka dot dress. Smart, white collar. Lacy. A little scratchy—stop fussing, she'd say, leave it alone. Red satin ribbon tied around my waist. Big bow at the back. All silky and shiny with a petticoat underneath, making a scrunch, scrunch noise. That sound … Mum made that dress. I think. Or one of my aunts. Someone made it. I loved it. I'd spin, I'd always spin in that

dress. You know when you spin so much you fall on the ground and it keeps moving and you think you'll never stand straight again … She gave that dress away when I got too big for it. I didn't want her to, I said I'll keep it and give it to my daughter when I have one but she didn't let me…

EMMA *returns to the room to collect her laptop ... but something about* BETH*'s story or voice (or both) makes her stop. And she watches, listens, unseen by the others.*

Anyway, I'm in the garden and I'm under the peppermint tree and I'm wearing my red polka dot dress and the sun is coming through the branches and making all these dapples of light and it looks so pretty in the photo but I'm not looking at the light because—I can see it coming up behind her … this shape, this figure … and I know I've got to keep in the shadows, I don't want it to see me in the light … but she keeps saying 'stand in the light' … For the photo, you see, and I can't tell her that it's coming, I can't find the words, they're locked in the back of my throat, it's coming … and I don't want to frighten her so I just keep still and keep my eye on it and Mum, she's shouting now, she's yelling at me—'I'll miss the light'—'I want to get you in the light'—'Look at me'—'Look'—but I can't take my eyes off it … She sighs and snaps the photo anyway and walks away … leaves me there and as soon as she's gone it snatches me up and carries me in its arms and I'm kicking and screaming but no-one hears me, no-one sees and I know that's it and Mum—Mum … I think that's the day she takes that photo …

EMMA: What photo?

BETH: She framed it and hung it on the wall. She said she liked the way the light looked like it was chasing me into the corner.

EMMA: Mum?

GRACE: You okay, Nan?

BETH: It's alright. It's alright.

EMMA: Mum?

BETH: I was just telling a story.

EMMA: Sure …

BETH: You're not the only one who can tell stories.

EMMA: We know.

Pause

BETH: Aren't you having a bath?

EMMA: I'm getting a drink.

BETH: But you've ordered—

EMMA: I don't care.

> EMMA *finds one of those small bottles of champagne in the mini-bar.*

BETH: Extravagant.

EMMA: What is?

BETH: Champagne and a bath. Thinks she's a movie star now.

EMMA: No I don't.

GRACE: It's a special weekend, Nan.

EMMA: I'm just trying to relax.

BETH: Hmm.

EMMA: What?

BETH: Nothing. Nothing …

> EMMA *heads back to the bathroom.*

GRACE: What was that about?

BETH: Let me brush your hair.

GRACE: Um, Nan?

BETH: Come here, come here, you look a fright.

GRACE: You've already brushed my hair.

BETH: Yes, I know, I know, I have but it isn't, it isn't …

GRACE: You can do it again, if you like?

BETH: You have awful hair.

GRACE: Nan!

BETH: It's just mess, messy all the time. Emma's was the same. Big, fat knots, right here. Awful.

> BETH *brushes* GRACE's *hair*

GRACE: I've missed you.

BETH: You're the one who moved away.

GRACE: I know.

BETH: I'm the one who stayed. I'm always the one who stayed …

GRACE: It's not forever.

BETH: I could have lived in Paris. Did you know that?

GRACE: Yeah, you've said.

BETH: J'adore Paris …

> BETH *falls into another world, for a moment. A pause.*

GRACE: I think she's avoiding me.

BETH: Hm?

GRACE: Emma. She's avoiding me.

BETH: Oh, no, I don't think so—

GRACE: Stuff it—why don't we go out?

BETH: It's cold. And dark. And I haven't had even had breakfast yet.

GRACE: We'll get all bundled up and go get hot chocolate and—and do whatever the hell we want. It's beautiful out there, Nan. It'll be like walking around in a book.

BETH: A book?

GRACE: Like the pages of a picture book or—or something—

BETH: Maybe later.

GRACE: Promise?

BETH: Yes.

GRACE: Do you want me to make you a cup of tea or coffee or something?

BETH: No.

GRACE: I can. I don't mind.

BETH: I think … I think everyone's just doing their best, don't you think?

GRACE: Sure they are.

BETH: Even Emma.

GRACE: Is she?

BETH: This is a big weekend for her.

GRACE: That's why I'm here, Nan, to support her, cheer her on.

BETH: I don't think she needs cheering on.

GRACE: That's exactly what Emma said.

BETH: Maybe she was right, maybe it could have waited.

GRACE: What?

BETH: Maybe this wasn't the right time, love. I'm sorry.

> *Beat.*

Perhaps we should have gone to Bali.

GRACE: We weren't invited.

BETH: Meh. Who'd want to go to Bali anyway?

GRACE: I would. I love Bali.

BETH: Maybe I would have gone, once, a long time ago, before all the tourists turned up and ruined it.

The doorbell rings.

GRACE: Room service! I'll get it.

GRACE *races to the door.* BETH *waits.*

SCENE FOUR

EMMA. *Alone. She is lying, flat out, on the floor. Similar position to* GRACE *when she lay out on the floor. The room grows darker around her.*

GRACE *enters, bursting through the front door. The light returns to the room.*

GRACE: Emma?

EMMA: [*not moving*] What?

GRACE: You alright?

EMMA: I'm writing.

GRACE: Oh. Really?

EMMA: It's part of the process.

GRACE: I do that. When I'm overwhelmed.

EMMA: —

GRACE: Lay out on the floor.

EMMA: —

GRACE: It's kinda weird but it just helps, doesn't it? Feels like everything stops moving, just for a moment, you're back in control.

Beat.

I forgot my camera.

Beat.

I know, I know, most people use their phones but I still like having a camera. Just feels better. Somehow. Like more legit or something. And the photos are better. I mean, maybe if I had a new phone the photos would turn out okay. I mean, people make movies with them now. Can you believe that? You couldn't do that with my phone. Have you seen my phone? It's terrible. So old. But I can't really be trusted with a new one. I know I'll break the screen. Drop it and smash it to pieces. So, what's the point?

EMMA: [*getting up*] Where's your nan?

GRACE: She found a lolly shop.

EMMA: Oh no.

GRACE: I know.

EMMA: You shouldn't leave her alone.

GRACE: She's fine.

EMMA: Hm.

GRACE: She is.

EMMA: You say that now …

GRACE: We're waiting for it to snow.

EMMA: Oh.

GRACE: Sat there for ages with our hot chocolates. Just waiting and waiting. Tricking ourselves into thinking the rain was turning into powder but it wasn't, it was just rain. Do you think it will though?

EMMA: What? Snow?

GRACE: We want to be out there when it happens.

EMMA: I think they're saying it won't.

GRACE: Oh … That's … She'll be disappointed.

EMMA: They could be wrong.

GRACE: Well, we're just going to wander now. Wander and hope for snow.

EMMA: Sounds nice.

GRACE: Sure you don't want to come?

EMMA: This isn't a holiday, not for me—

GRACE: It could be.

EMMA: It's not.

GRACE: There's hours before your lecture.

EMMA: I can't.

GRACE: Because you're writing?

    Beat.

I read your stories to the kids, the kids I teach.

EMMA: Oh.

GRACE: They love them.

EMMA: I'm sure they'd prefer Harry Potter or something but, that's— that's nice to hear.

GRACE: They're little shits.

EMMA: Are they?

GRACE: But I like them.

EMMA: I'm sure they like you, too.

GRACE: I told them I'd get them postcards.

EMMA: Okay.

GRACE: All of them. Not just one for the class. No, no, no, that would have been too easy. No, I told them I'd get all of them their very own postcard.

Beat.

Need to find twenty-five different postcards.

Beat.

I don't mind. Not really. They were pretty excited. For me. Coming here, you know? Most of them haven't ever left the country. Even though it's so close. Europe, I mean.

EMMA: Yeah, right …

GRACE: I want to try to get each of them a postcard that matches their personalities.

EMMA: Sounds like you've got a lot of work to do.

GRACE: I do. I also have to get something for the twins.

EMMA: I'm sure you don't have to do that.

GRACE: I promised them.

EMMA: So. How old are they now? Six? Seven?

GRACE: Ten.

EMMA: Ten? Wow. Really?

GRACE: You wouldn't even recognise them.

EMMA: No, probably not.

GRACE: You've never seen them, never visited them—

EMMA: No.

GRACE: I think it'd make them happy. If you did. Sometime.

EMMA: I really should get back to …

GRACE: What are you working on?

EMMA: Nothing. I mean. Nothing I can really talk about. Not yet.

GRACE: You don't really talk much. Anymore.

EMMA: What?

GRACE: You used to talk and talk and talk.

EMMA: Did I?

GRACE: Amazing.

EMMA: Sorry?

GRACE: Nothing.

EMMA: Your nan is probably starting to get worried—

GRACE: I wish you'd come with us.

EMMA: I can't.

GRACE: It's a beautiful day out there.

EMMA: You said it's raining.

GRACE: Yeah, it is drizzling. Don't you love that?

EMMA: You'll just have to take photos for me.

GRACE: Just come.

EMMA: I think—I mean, I might have an idea, for a new book, actually.

GRACE: Oh yeah?

EMMA: It's about fairies. They're everywhere but they're small, so you can't see them. They're so tiny they ride around on the backs of mosquitoes.

GRACE: Really?

EMMA: Maybe not mosquitoes. No-one likes mosquitoes. It could be dragonflies but I feel like that's been done and … and anyway, these tiny fairies are everywhere and we humans, we can't see them—but we can see the things they do, the stuff they leave behind, like the ripples they leave behind in puddles.

GRACE: I know that story.

EMMA: What?

GRACE: That's my story.

EMMA: —

GRACE: You told me that story. You don't remember?

EMMA: No, I—I don't—

GRACE: We were sitting on my bed, looking out my window, waiting for the rain to stop. You don't remember this?

EMMA: Maybe, I don't know, I—

GRACE: I was maybe five or six. Little. Had that creepy pink bear I carried around everywhere, you remember that? Anyway, I'd been throwing a tantrum because Mum wouldn't let me outside in the rain and you came in and told me that story. About the fairies in the puddles. Rain fairies. That's what I called them.

EMMA: Rain fairies?

GRACE: Yeah.

EMMA: You liked it? That story?

GRACE: To be honest I liked anything you did back then. You could have been reading me articles from the *Financial Times* and I would have thought it was the most wonderous thing I'd ever heard.

EMMA: Oh.

GRACE: But I loved it. It stayed with me. Forever.

Pause

EMMA: So, I'd better … get back to it …

GRACE: Sure. Okay …

GRACE *picks up her camera.*

Could I … take a photo … before I …

EMMA: Of me?

GRACE: Yeah. If that's—is that weird?

EMMA: Um.

GRACE: I don't have to.

EMMA: No, no, it's—um, fine, where, where should I?

GRACE: Don't pose.

EMMA: No?

GRACE: Just be natural.

EMMA: Oh god.

GRACE: Act like I'm not even here.

EMMA: Ah. Right. Maybe, I'll, I'll sit? Is that—

GRACE: Yeah, yeah, that's good.

GRACE *takes the photo.*

EMMA: All done?

GRACE: All done.

EMMA: Okay?

GRACE: You look beautiful.

EMMA: Oh. No, no, I don't—I don't think so.

GRACE: See you at the lecture?

EMMA: Sure.

GRACE *exits.* EMMA, *alone, takes a moment before returning to the floor.*

SCENE FIVE

GRACE *is sleeping on the sofa.*

EMMMA *enters through the front door, quietly. She watches* GRACE.

GRACE *stirs.*

EMMA: Sorry.

GRACE: Shit … Sorry.

EMMA: Didn't mean to wake you.

GRACE: Everything okay?

EMMA: Yeah, yeah.

> *Silence*

GRACE: Are you drunk?

EMMA: No.

GRACE: Tipsy?

EMMA: No.

GRACE: What time is it?

EMMA: It's late.

GRACE: Where were you?

EMMA: They took me out—

GRACE: We waited up for you.

EMMA: I sent a message.

GRACE: Did you?

EMMA: I thought I …

GRACE: Good night?

EMMA: Not really.

GRACE: Oh.

EMMA: Publishers, producers, agents, all pretending they like me.

GRACE: Maybe they do.

EMMA: Do what?

GRACE: Like you.

EMMA: Of course they do. Some of them. I'm being dramatic.

GRACE: I get dramatic when I'm drunk, too.

EMMA: I'm not drunk.

GRACE: We had mulled wine.

EMMA: Did you?

GRACE: We wore our beanies and coats and gloves and drank mulled wine on the street and I think I want to live here now forever.

EMMA: It's only because you're on holiday.

GRACE: I know.

EMMA: It's not real.

GRACE: Your lecture was good.

EMMA: Thanks.

GRACE: Yeah, really good, super interesting.

EMMA: 'The Importance of Children's Literature in the Twenty-First Century'

GRACE: I know. I was there.

EMMA: I saw you. Sitting dead centre with your nan.

GRACE: We had good seats—

EMMA: She looked petrified. She always looks so petrified. You noticed that?

GRACE: She was a bit nervous.

EMMA: So was I.

GRACE: You didn't seem it.

EMMA: Good. That's …

GRACE: She was really proud of you.

EMMA: She said that?

GRACE: We tried to find you after but—

EMMA: You sure you're comfortable, because I could ask for a trundle / bed or something—

GRACE: No, no, really, this is good, it's really good.

EMMA: And you're warm enough? Need an extra blanket?

GRACE: I'm good. This is good.

EMMA: Sorry I woke you.

She goes to leave.

GRACE: Emma?

EMMA: Yeah?

GRACE: Nothing …

EMMA: [*going to exit*] Good night, Grace.

GRACE: I've written something.

EMMA: [*stopping*] Sorry?

GRACE: I've written something.

EMMA: What?

GRACE: I've written / something

EMMA: No, no I mean what—what have you written?

GRACE: A story.

EMMA: Okay.

GRACE: About you.

EMMA: What?

GRACE: I mean sort of, not really, not directly—like you're the inspiration or actually not even that, so much, I mean you're more just—just nothing. It's nothing. Really, it's nothing—I, I shouldn't have even brought it up.

EMMA: You want me to read it?

GRACE: No.

EMMA: I don't mind.

GRACE: Um.

EMMA: People ask me to read their stuff all the time.

GRACE: You don't need to.

EMMA: I know I don't need to, I want to. For you.

GRACE: You do?

EMMA: Of course.

GRACE: Really?

EMMA: Jesus, I wouldn't have offered if I / didn't want to—

GRACE: I just wanted it to be a surprise. You know?

EMMA: No.

GRACE: Like when you saw it, out there, in the world.

EMMA: What are you talking about.

GRACE: They're publishing it.

EMMA: Your story?

GRACE: Yes.

EMMA: Your story about me?

GRACE: It's not really about you.

EMMA: Yeah, yeah, you said.

GRACE: It's a novel.

EMMA: So not a story?

GRACE: A story is a novel, isn't it?

EMMA: Not necessarily.

GRACE: Okay. Well this is a novel and a story.

EMMA: Right.

GRACE: And they're really excited about it.

EMMA: Who's they?

GRACE: Harper Collins.

EMMA: Really?

GRACE: I got an advance.

EMMA: You did?

GRACE: It's coming out in the summer.

EMMA: And it's about me?

GRACE: Not / really—

EMMA: Inspired by me.

GRACE: No, no, I meant, I mean you inspired me to write it.

EMMA: Great.

GRACE: Cos I was journaling, you know about journaling?

EMMA: I get the idea.

GRACE: You should try it. It's good for mindfulness.

EMMA: Mindfulness?

GRACE: Anyway, I was doing that and the story—

EMMA: Novel.

GRACE: Well, yeah, but it wasn't, it wasn't a novel then, it was a story and it just sort of spilled out of me.

EMMA: Spilled?

GRACE: That's probably not the / right word..

EMMA: No, it's good, it's good.

GRACE: The head teacher read it—

EMMA: At your school.

GRACE: My boss.

EMMA: She have an eye for that sort of thing does she?

GRACE: She's connected.

EMMA: To?

GRACE: Her friend is Denise Cassidy, do you know Denise? At Harper?

EMMA: No.

GRACE: Well, she gave it to her and next thing it was all just happening.

EMMA: That easy?

GRACE: It wasn't easy.

EMMA: But it wasn't a struggle was it?

GRACE: Um.

EMMA: This is the first thing you wrote?

GRACE: Kinda.

EMMA: Jesus.

GRACE: I mean, no, no, I've written things, other / things, I have—

EMMA: Congratulations.

GRACE: Thanks.

EMMA: You must be excited.

GRACE: I am.

EMMA: Not much money in it. You know that, right?

GRACE: Money in?

EMMA: Being an author.

GRACE: I'm not an author.

EMMA: You wrote a book?

GRACE: Yeah.

EMMA: You're an author.

GRACE: Okay, yeah, but I mean—not like you. You write proper books / that mean something

EMMA: So yours isn't a proper book?

GRACE: Not like yours are.

EMMA: I write for children, is your book for children?

GRACE: No.

EMMA: Well, your book would be considered a more 'proper book' than mine already.

GRACE: Don't say that.

EMMA: I write about talking animals.

GRACE: So did George Orwell.

EMMA: My animals aren't talking about Stalinism.

GRACE: The one-eared rabbit.

EMMA: Yeah, nothing about that one that's particularly earth shattering.

GRACE: And the dragon with no fire.

EMMA: Right, again, just a story—

GRACE: Not just a story, it's more than—

EMMA: You just going to list them all, are you?

GRACE: No, I just—they're special, that's all. Your books are special.

EMMA: Don't know about that.

GRACE: And not just to me, to heaps of people.

EMMA: That's very kind. Thank you.

GRACE: I'd always thought you'd written them for me.

EMMA: Oh.

GRACE: But you didn't?

EMMA: They're for children and you were a child, so I suppose they were for you, in a way.

GRACE: Ruby the Forgotten Mouse.

EMMA: What about her?

GRACE: That wasn't me?

EMMA: It's a mouse.

GRACE: Mum always said that you'd wanted me to have my very own story, and that one, Ruby, that was mine.

EMMA: It's a mouse.

GRACE: It's an allegory.

EMMA: No, it's not. I mean, it's nice, it's flattering that you think I'm that clever but I'm not, not really. It was just a story—

GRACE: I don't believe you.

EMMA: There's nothing deep or magical or—or whatever it is that you or Sophie or your grandmother have dreamed up. It's a story. I made it up. I wrote it down. I can't control what people turn it into, that's not my fault.

GRACE: Fault? No-one is saying anything is your fault.

BETH *enters*

BETH: It's the middle of the bloody night.

GRACE: Sorry, Nan.

BETH: I always found her a bit whiny.

EMMA: What are you talking about?

BETH: Ruby. The whiny bloody mouse.

EMMA: What?

BETH: That's what you two were arguing about, wasn't it?

EMMA: We weren't arguing.

BETH: The little mouse. Squeak. Squeak. Squeak. All alone and frightened.

EMMA: That's not how it goes.

BETH: The little mouse. Squeak. Squeak. Squeak.

EMMA: Mum—

BETH: A whiny, pain in the arse / mouse—

GRACE: I liked her.

BETH: You would.

GRACE: Nan!

BETH: What?

GRACE: Millions of kids liked her, still like her—

EMMA: Grace is publishing a book.

BETH: What? No, she isn't.

GRACE: I am.

BETH: Everyone's publishing a bloody book these days.

GRACE: Yeah, well—

EMMA: She's writing about me.

BETH: Sorry?

EMMA: Her book. It's about me.

GRACE: No, it's not. Not really.

EMMA: [*to* BETH] Did you know about this?

BETH: Not at all. Grace, what's going on?

EMMA: She's writing about me and she's come here, unannounced, for some more backstory. Is that it? Editor questioning some of the holes in the plot?

GRACE: No!

BETH: Grace, what's going on?

GRACE: That's not it—that's not what I … I have written a novel. You inspired me. That's it.

EMMA: Sure.

GRACE: I don't see what the big deal is, seriously. It's just a book.

EMMA: I'm a private person, Grace, and I'd appreciate it if I could keep it that way.

GRACE: It's my story.

EMMA: But you're here to get my permission. Isn't that what all this is about?

GRACE: No, that's—that's not—I don't need your permission. This is my story.

EMMA: I know how this works, Grace.

GRACE: Do you?

BETH: Darling, I don't think you understand—

GRACE: This my story. My book. My writing. Mine.

BETH: Disney are going to turn her books into films. Films!

Pause

GRACE: Are you joking?

EMMA: No.

GRACE: Disney?

EMMA: I hope so—

GRACE: Oh my god. That's perfect, that is fucking perfect.

EMMA: What's the problem?

GRACE: You'd sell out to the highest bidder. Give up those beautiful stories for what? What?

EMMA: I'm not selling out—

GRACE: You hate that shit.

EMMA: What shit?

GRACE: Disney shit.

EMMA: No I don't, why does everyone keep saying that?

GRACE: Those books can't be Disney films—

EMMA: I haven't got anything else. Nothing. This is it. This is my chance—

GRACE: That's bullshit.

BETH: She hasn't written a thing in over ten years.

EMMA: Yeah, Mum, we all know, everyone knows.

BETH: She needs this deal.

GRACE: So? Get the deal? It's got nothing to do with me.

EMMA: But your book is about me.

GRACE: Fuck! Not everything's about you! You haven't read it—you've got no idea.

EMMA: It's not good timing.

GRACE: Sorry it doesn't fit your timeline, your schedule, but it's my story, my book deal, my fucking life and it's happening whether you support it or not.

EMMA: You have no right, Grace, no right at all—

GRACE: I thought you'd be fucking proud of me for once, just once and maybe, maybe it was something we could celebrate, together, all of us, and I'm sorry I said anything. I shouldn't have said anything …

> GRACE *exits quickly—to* BETH*'s room.*

> *Silence.*

BETH: Great, she's taken my room. Of course. Suppose this means I'm on the couch.

EMMA: Fucking hell.

BETH: Actually, you should take the couch.

EMMA: What the hell am I going to do?

BETH: I'll get a bad back if I try to sleep there.

EMMA: Mum.

BETH: I'm going to sleep in your bed.

EMMA: You told me she was happy, that she was thriving. You've said that. You've always said that.

BETH: Oh, she's fine.

EMMA: That did not seem like fine.

BETH: She's just going through that stage.

EMMA: What stage?

BETH: Teenagers are notorious for being over emotional. It's the hormones.

EMMA: She isn't a teenager.

BETH: Hmm?

EMMA: Grace. Grace isn't a teenager anymore.

BETH: No, no, of course, Grace is—she's ...

EMMA: You alright?

BETH: Yes, yes.

EMMA: Shit. I don't—I don't know how to speak to her.

BETH: Maybe because you're not telling her what she wants to hear.

EMMA: I don't know what to say, Mum.

BETH: Just talk to her. Talk. That's why she came.

EMMA: She's written a book. A book. That's just ... that's not good. That can't be good, can it?

BETH: Who knows?

EMMA: I know, Mum. I know.

BETH: We were in the caravan. All crowded in. Remember? You two sharing that bed in the annex. With the spiders. You were both so terrified of the spiders. It rained the whole time and we were freezing, absolutely freezing because we'd not brought any warm clothes. This was supposed to be our beach holiday. Our first one since ... But the weather was having none of it. So we went to that little op shop. Sophie wouldn't come in because she hated the way it smelled—moth balls and mould—but the smell didn't bother you. You were in there, rummaging through the crowded shelves, finding blankets and jumpers and books. So many books. I said, books won't keep us warm. And you—remember, you remember what you said …

EMMA *says nothing.*

BETH: You said, books warm the heart, Mummy.

EMMA: I didn't say it.

BETH: I remember it.

EMMA: Whatever you say.

BETH: No, you said it.

EMMA: Alright.

BETH: And when we went to the counter, all the books you'd chosen were for me and Sophie. There was nothing for you. You'd taken all that time choosing books for us and got nothing for yourself.

EMMA: Because I could make my own stories.

BETH: That's right.

EMMA: I don't think any of this is actually true.

BETH: It is.

EMMA: You've just told that story so many times you started to believe it.

BETH: What happened to her?

EMMA: Who?

BETH: That little girl.

EMMA: I don't think that little girl ever existed, Mum. I think she was always a figment of your imagination.

BETH: Don't say that.

EMMA: Sorry I haven't lived up to the five-year-old version of myself.

BETH: That's not what I mean.

EMMA: What do you mean, then?

Pause.

Mum? What did you mean?

BETH: You can't see it.

EMMA: See what?

BETH: You're more alike than you know.

EMMA: Who?

BETH: You and Grace.

EMMA: And?

BETH: Think about it.

EMMA: About what?

BETH: I don't know, Emma. I can't fix everything for you all the bloody time.

EMMA: What are you fixing exactly? What?

BETH: This. All of this. Mess.

EMMA: Then talk to Grace. Tell her she can't do this—

BETH: I don't think I was loving enough.

EMMA: What are you talking about?

BETH: For you and Soph—I wasn't, I wasn't maternal and whatnot, was I? I mean I never made scones for the cake stall or volunteered at the school canteen or whatever it was those other women did.

EMMA: How do you do that?

BETH: What have I done?

EMMA: Twist it and turn it so it always, somehow, comes back to you.

BETH: I don't do that.

EMMA: This isn't about you, Mum.

BETH: Don't think it's about you, either.

EMMA: Of course it is.

BETH: Perhaps it's about Grace.

EMMA: Which makes it about me.

BETH: You don't know that.

EMMA: I'm in her fucking book, Mum.

BETH: You need to stop worrying what people think.

EMMA: Oh my god.

BETH: You've always been like that.

EMMA: That's got nothing to do with—

BETH: Of course you got that from me. I should have been less— judgemental? Is that what I was?

EMMA: I can't talk to you right now.

BETH: I'm trying to help.

EMMA: Are you?

BETH: Yes. But I shouldn't have damn well bothered.

EMMA: Go to bed, Mum.

BETH: I think I will. Yes. I will.

> BETH *exits.* EMMA *takes off her shoes, sinks into the couch.*

SCENE SIX

BETH, *alone, finds a bottle of wine in the minibar. Pours a glass. Relaxes.*

After a moment, EMMA *enters. She carries a shopping bag.*

EMMA: Save any of that for me?
BETH: You want a glass?
EMMA: Is that from the mini-bar?
BETH: Not sure. Grace opened it.
EMMA: It's from the mini-bar.
BETH: Oh. Dear …
EMMA: Pour me one at least.
BETH: You got that space you needed?
EMMA: I did.
BETH: Anyone would think you're avoiding her.
EMMA: Maybe.
BETH: And me.
EMMA: Never … Where is she?
BETH: Out.
EMMA: I see / that—
BETH: [*referring to Emma's shopping*] What's that you've got there?
EMMA: Just bought something. For the ceremony.
BETH: Without me?
EMMA: It's not a big deal.
BETH: Yes, it is. Go try it on. Show me.
EMMA: Now?
BETH: You did try it on, didn't you?
EMMA: When?
BETH: In the store. Before you bought it.
EMMA: I know my size.
BETH: Emma.
EMMA: What?
BETH: You have to try it on.
EMMA: It will be fine.
BETH: Then show me, go on, try it on.
EMMA: [*as she exits*] Jesus Christ, mother. Alright, alright, I'll try it on.

BETH: Remember when you and Sophie would do those god-awful fashion shows?

EMMA: [*off*] No.

BETH: Yes, you do. They were terrible. You'd both look so serious. Cheeks sucked in. That stupid walk. God. It was boring. Watching you walk up and down the living room. Wondered what the hell I'd created. My daughters. The models. Ugh.

EMMA: [*off*] Sophie wanted to be a model. Not me.

BETH: Sophie probably could have been a model.

EMMA: [*off*] Thanks a lot, Mum.

BETH: Don't think that's a compliment.

EMMA: [*off*] It is.

BETH: Hurry up.

> EMMA *emerges in a dress. It's not bad but it's not ... great.*

That, that's what you're going to wear?

EMMA: It's quite a low-key event so ...

BETH: It's a banquet.

EMMA: Yes.

BETH: A banquet isn't particularly low-key.

EMMA: It's not—it's not the Oscars.

BETH: So, you're wearing that?

EMMA: Well, after that reaction …

BETH: What? What did I say?

EMMA: Your face, look at your face.

BETH: My face isn't doing anything.

EMMA: Yes, it is.

BETH: Well, it is now because you're making it.

EMMA: You hate it.

BETH: I don't hate it. It's just—it's just a little, beige. A little bland. Boring.

EMMA: Great.

BETH: Wear it. You don't look bad.

EMMA: No. I look bland. I think that's even worse.

BETH: What else have you got?

EMMA: Nothing.

BETH: You must have brought something with you. I know you, Emma. There's a dress in your bag right now isn't there.

EMMA: No.

BETH: You brought one over with you, decided you hate it and went out and bought … that …

EMMA: Fuck's sake.

BETH: I'm right.

EMMA: Perhaps.

BETH: Put it on.

EMMA: I don't like it. It isn't right.

BETH: Show me.

EMMA: Mum—

BETH: I'll be honest.

EMMA: That's the problem.

BETH: Go, go, put it on for me.

> EMMA *goes to her room to change.*

EMMA: [*off*] Jesus Christ, mother…

BETH: Should I paint my nails?

EMMA: [*off*] If you want—

BETH: Bright red, I'd like them to be bright red.

EMMA: [*off*] I didn't bring any nail polish.

BETH: Don't mind doing it, but I hate taking it off. The smell of that remover. Nail polish remover. You know that smell, don't you? Hate it. End up just picking it off, scraping it off with a knife, the polish, the red, but then you end up with these … I don't bother. My mother always did. Not always red. She had a whole rainbow of colours. Could you imagine? Different colour on each nail if you wanted …I only really like red. Bright red. Do you think I …

EMMA: [*off*] Mum? Are you okay?

BETH: Mum could never do her right hand. I'd help her with that. When I was bigger, of course, not when I … And she'd lay out some old magazine on the table and spread her fingers wide and she had his heavy musk perfume and her floral dressing gown. Silk. Hair in rollers. Like a movie star in her trailer, you know and I'd try so hard not to shake. Those brushes are really tiny, you know, delicate because, well, nails are small and you're only meant to do one stroke down the middle then one side then the other side. Little brush. And I'd shake and I could feel her staring, you know. Her eyes would get real small and sharp. Couldn't look at her. Concentrating on the … but I could feel it and I'd try so hard because I … Had this bright red polish on the brush and missed her nail and got it all down her finger and …

Silence.

She drinks her wine. Maybe she finishes the glass.

EMMA *re-enters in the new dress.*

EMMA: Mum? What are you doing?

BETH: Oh, nothing, just, just thinking.

EMMA: You alright?

BETH: Yes, yes, let me get a look at you.

EMMA: Here it is!

BETH: See, that looks so much better.

EMMA: Better?

BETH: Yes, better. In that other thing you looked like a middle-aged woman.

EMMA: I am a middle-aged woman.

BETH: It is a celebration, Emma, you might as well dress up for it a bit.

EMMA: I feel ridiculous.

BETH: You look lovely.

EMMA: You hate it.

BETH: I don't hate it.

EMMA: But?

BETH: It's—um—classy. You look very professional.

EMMA: Oh god.

BETH: Stop it. You look lovely. You're wearing that one. I demand it. More wine?

EMMA: You have to slow down …

BETH: It's not looking good, so I may as well enjoy it. Go out with a bang.

EMMA: What are you talking about?

BETH: Me. I'm talking about me. I am falling apart.

EMMA: You're too young to be falling apart.

BETH: That's why you brought me here, isn't it? A final hurrah.

EMMA: No, Mum.

BETH: Paris would have been a more suitable choice.

EMMA: Again. I am sorry.

BETH: Did you want to see what I'm wearing?

EMMA: No.

BETH: I bought it specially and everything. Sophie helped me choose it.

EMMA: Did she?

BETH: Don't be jealous. You despise shopping.

EMMA: I do.

BETH: [*as she exits*] You won't get the full effect, because there's earrings too—

EMMA: Earrings?

BETH: [*off*] Yes, matching earrings. I went all out.

EMMA: [*to herself*] I'm sure you did.

BETH: [*off*] It had been so long since I'd bought myself a new frock.

EMMA: Frock?

BETH: [*off*] You'll have to help with the zip.

EMMA: Come out.

BETH: Hang on, hang on.

As EMMA *waits, she picks up a journal and starts flicking through the pages. It's* GRACE*'s journal. She closes it quickly. Puts it down.*

EMMA: [*towards the other room*] Can you ask Grace to keep the place tidy?

BETH: [*off*] Ask her yourself.

EMMA *returns to the journal, finds one page in particular of interest. She reads with one eye on the door to her mother's room.*

Finally, BETH *makes her entrance in a stunning red dress.*

Isn't it gorgeous?

It is. But it is also far too much, too over the top, too glamourous— EMMA *looks even more beige beside her mother. She takes a moment.*

Do me up, do me up.

EMMA *does.*

Nice, huh?

EMMA: You look beautiful.

BETH: I love it.

EMMA: Good.

BETH: Twenty-one-year-old me hated myself for this. Shopping for a fancy dress to wear to some fancy event. So bourgeois. That's what I would have said.

EMMA: You've earned the right to be a little bourgeois now and then, Mum.

BETH: I love it.

EMMA: You've said.

BETH: [*noticing the journal*] You were reading that?

EMMA: No. I wasn't.

BETH: I don't care if you were.

EMMA: I wasn't.

BETH: Trying to get a sneak peek of her novel.

EMMA: I don't give a shit about her novel.

BETH: Don't get jealous, it's not attractive.

EMMA: I'm not jealous.

BETH: Of course you are. You've never written a novel.

EMMA: Has she shown you? Have you read it?

BETH: No.

EMMA: She can't write about me. She doesn't know me.

BETH: That's the problem, I think.

EMMA: I don't know what to do.

BETH: Look, the chances are, no-one is going to even read the thing.

EMMA: Harper Collins, Mum. She's been published by Harper fucking Collins.

BETH: Big deal.

EMMA: It's a huge deal!

BETH: I think you're getting a little ahead of yourself—

EMMA: It will be out there. What a story. They'll have a field day with it, won't they? Children's author gives up own child. Abandons baby daughter.

BETH: But it wasn't like that.

EMMA: I gave her up.

BETH: Yes—

EMMA: That's what they'll boil it down to. They don't care about the nuances or the reasons, do they?

BETH: They?

EMMA: Mothers. They judge. They do. You know they will.

BETH: I—

EMMA: They watch, wait, ready to pounce on any little thing, any little, tiny thing. And they will pounce like a lioness, they will pounce on me and tear me to shreds because I dared—dared to do what they didn't have the guts to do, or to say or to even let themselves think. And you think Disney or any of them are going to want to go near me once those mothers have dug their claws in?

BETH: We don't know that.

EMMA: What the hell is she thinking? Writing something like that.

BETH: You don't know what she's written.

EMMA: Oh, I know, I know, why else did she turn up? Why else is she here?

BETH: To see you.

EMMA: Why now? Why?

BETH: I thought it would be a good idea.

EMMA: Thanks, Mum. What a great fucking idea.

BETH: You should have made more of an effort.

EMMA: I did.

BETH: When?

EMMA: I tried. You know, I tried.

BETH: You should have been there, a little more, don't you think?

EMMA: Why are you telling me this now? What is the fucking point?

BETH: I've had some wine.

EMMA: I can tell.

BETH: Look, I think we've all made mistakes and—

EMMA: The mistake was having her. I knew it wasn't right. I knew. Before she was even born. I knew I didn't want it … But Sophie … Sophie is a beautiful mother. Beautiful. Any child who ends up with someone like that for a mother is fucking lucky. I'm not that. I'm not Sophie. And I didn't—I don't want to be. I couldn't.

BETH: Yes, well—

EMMA: Would you stop pulling that face. Stop it.

BETH: I'm not.

EMMA: You are.

BETH: I loved being a mother. I didn't think I would. I mean, I was adamant I wasn't going to have children—

EMMA: I know, you've told me, many times—

BETH: But oops, it happened and—and I was pissed off about it, so pissed off. Especially with you. I'd been through it. I'd done it. I didn't think I wanted to do it again. Then, when you were born and when I held you in my arms … it was … it was everything … you were everything …

EMMA: Okay.

BETH: I thought it would be the same for you.

EMMA: …

BETH: So I forced you.

EMMA: No you didn't.

BETH: Thought you'd regret it. That's all. Didn't want you to feel that regret, didn't want you to get old and wish for something that couldn't be … and … well …

EMMA: I don't regret it. I don't regret what I did.

BETH: They'd probably prefer it if you did.

EMMA: Who?

BETH: All of them.

EMMA: You?

BETH: Yes. If I'm honest. Yes.

Silence. EMMA *can't look at her mother. She is so, desperately, hurt.*

BETH: I think I'd like to go home now.

EMMA: You can't.

BETH: I shouldn't be here.

EMMA: Mum!

BETH: You could make things better, in an instant, in a second but instead, you—you—you just—

EMMA: I did make it better. Everything I did was to make it better.

BETH: Then why isn't it?

EMMA: I couldn't stay because I was in the way. And I couldn't leave because that was selfish. And if I was happy I was evil. But if I was sad I was ungrateful. Nothing I did was right. Nothing I did was enough.

BETH: So you just gave up.

EMMA: I didn't belong. I didn't deserve to belong. But I also didn't deserve to leave.

BETH: So dramatic.

EMMA: I'm trying to explain.

BETH: I never asked for an explanation.

EMMA: That's it. That's it, right there. You never asked. You never ask. Because you don't give a shit about anything or anyone except yourself. It's all about you. It's all about your suffering and your regrets and you can't see how, for one second, your own children might also be suffering. Might also have regrets. Might need a fucking mother to actually be there for them and act like they give a shit about. To love them. To turn up and be a part of their lives. To be proud of them.

    GRACE *enters, interrupting them. She clocks the tension.*

GRACE: Oh my god. Nan. You look amazing.

BETH: Oh. Stop.

GRACE: You do, Nan. Incredible. Stunning.

BETH: That's the reaction I was hoping from this one.

EMMA: What? I said you looked beautiful.

GRACE: She does. You do, Nan. Beautiful.

BETH: It's for tomorrow night.

GRACE: It's really lovely. What are you going to wear, Emma?

EMMA: This.

GRACE: Oh. That's nice, too.

EMMA: Is it?

BETH: Be honest with her, Grace.

GRACE: It's very um sophisticated.

EMMA: Sophisticated?

GRACE: Plain but, but nice plain, you know?

BETH: Plain is the word.

EMMA: You should probably stop—

GRACE: Sorry, I didn't mean—

BETH: I should get out of this—

GRACE: [*to* BETH] Do you need a hand with the zip?

BETH: Um, yes, I, yes, I do, I will, please …

GRACE: Yeah, I can—

BETH: Oh … oh shit …for fuck's sake …

> BETH *has wet herself.*

GRACE: It's alright, Nan, I'll sort it out, don't worry, don't worry—

BETH: Don't touch me—

GRACE: [*exiting to bathroom*] I'll get a towel.

EMMA: [*exiting with* GRACE *to bathroom*] No, no, I'll get paper, just paper…

> BETH *is alone. Quiet. She stands very, very still. Like she is afraid. As if moving will somehow make it worse.*

> EMMA *and* GRACE *return.*

EMMA: Mum?

BETH: I've ruined it, haven't I? My dress. Ruined it. I have. / I have. I have. I have.

EMMA: It's alright, Mum, Really. Come on. Let's get you out of it and we can—

BETH: Don't.

EMMA: Mum, it's alright.

BETH: It's not alright. It's fucking—it's, / it's

EMMA: We can get it dry-cleaned, they do that sort of thing so quickly now, a couple of hours, that's all and it will be good as new and—

BETH: I'm so ashamed.

EMMA: It's only me. You've got nothing to be ashamed of. Nothing. Ever. Ever. Come on. We'll get this all fixed up. Come on.

> *This time* BETH *lets her daughter take her.* EMMA *guides* BETH *to the other room.*

> GRACE *cleans up the floor. Silence.*

> EMMA *returns.*

GRACE: Is she okay?

EMMA: She wants to be alone.

GRACE: Oh, yeah, right, of course.

EMMA: [*referring to the clean-up*] I can do that.

GRACE: It's okay, I got it.

EMMA: Let me help, at least.

GRACE: Really, it's fine. It's nothing.

GRACE *speaks as she finishes the clean-up.* EMMA *hovers, unsure and feeling a little useless.*

GRACE: You sure she's alright?

EMMA: She's gone to have a shower.

GRACE: Oh, yeah, right, okay.

Pause

EMMA: So, um, you're in the UK now?

GRACE: Yep.

EMMA: London is / quite—

GRACE: Manchester.

EMMA: Oh, yes, that's right, you said … You like it?

GRACE: I don't hate it.

EMMA: That's something.

GRACE: Yeah.

Pause

EMMA: I lived in London. When I was about your age.

GRACE: I know.

EMMA: Oh. You said you lived with some friends, didn't you?

GRACE: I don't really feel like making small talk right now.

Silence.

EMMA: Look, I need—I need to ask you not to publish this. Yet. Not yet. Until I've signed. With Disney. I just need this contract.

Beat.

It's just—this—this book you're writing, it might—it might change some, some perceptions out there, about me, which means I could … what's the (word) … you know, I might—I could lose some of my box office appeal … This—your—book could fuck it all up for me.

GRACE: Since when do you care what people think?

EMMA: Grace, I'm asking you to please just hold off.

GRACE: I can't. It's all locked in.

EMMA: Surely you could—

GRACE: Where have you been?

EMMA: Sorry?

GRACE: It doesn't—it doesn't matter.

EMMA: I haven't kept in touch like I should, I know that, I know—

GRACE: Fourteen years.

EMMA: I know.

GRACE: You were there. I mean, not all the time but you were around. For the big things and sometimes just for dinner or whatever and it wasn't perfect but it was okay, it worked, didn't it? Like I knew it was weird cos I had you and Mum—Sophie—and other kids just had one mum, but … but really I felt lucky … I felt like I was a bit special. Different to the others. In a good way. You know?

EMMA: It was a long / time ago

GRACE: Anyway, I thought it worked and I was fine, I was happy and—I don't remember when it happened, like the date or whatever but it was like, you just stopped. You didn't come round. You just weren't there anymore.

EMMA: It was complicated.

GRACE: Enlighten me.

EMMA: You know all this. Sophie has told you. Your nan has told you.

> GRACE *says nothing.*

I had some opportunities and I had to take them.

GRACE: You left me behind.

EMMA: I did not.

> *Beat.*

You had your life, your family, your home, your …

> *Beat.*

And, I—I didn't leave you. Sophie took you. It's very different.

> *Beat.*

She is wonderful mother. You know that don't you? I mean, anyone would be lucky to / have—

GRACE: I know.

> *Silence*

EMMA: I didn't not want you. I just didn't want to be a mother. Does that make sense?

GRACE: No.

EMMA: It might, one day.

GRACE: How about something that makes sense today?

EMMA: Okay. I'm a selfish, shallow, self-absorbed bitch who deserves to be burned at the stake for her crimes.

GRACE: —

EMMA: You know I never wanted to hurt you.

Beat.

I did the best thing for you.

GRACE: You did the best thing for you.

EMMA: For both of us.

GRACE: You didn't have to disappear completely.

EMMA: I did.

GRACE: Who said?

EMMA: We can't change it now, Grace.

GRACE: But we can.

BETH: [*off*] Emma!

EMMA: I'm sorry, I really have to check on her—

EMMA *goes to exit, hesitates ...*

EMMA: There was a mother. Watching over her baby.

GRACE: Sorry?

EMMA: I, um, I thought I could tell you a story.

GRACE: A story?

EMMA: It's stupid.

GRACE: No, no it's not. Please. I want to hear it.

EMMA: It's not mine. It's Hans Christian Andersen's story.

GRACE: Um, that's—that's okay.

EMMA: Right. So, um, the mother is watching over her baby. The baby won't stop crying and neither have slept. For days. And then, one night, a figure appears. It's Death but the mother doesn't know this yet. Death makes her feel at peace and for the first time in a long time, she can finally, finally fall asleep. But that's a mistake. Because the moment she closes her eyes, Death steals the baby from her. She chases after him, takes this long and difficult journey, goes through all these terrible, horrible tasks to prove her worth. And she does. And so, eventually, Death meets her. But he won't just give her the baby. No. Instead, he shows her the futures of two children. One of them has a happy, wonderful, fulfilled life. The other lives a life of misery, poverty, pain. He tells her one of those children is hers. One of those futures is the future of her baby. But he won't tell her which one. She can take back her child but it could end up living a life of misery and pain. Or maybe it wouldn't. Will she risk it? Risk giving that future to her child? It's her choice. Her choice … So … she turns her back, let's her child go with Death. Makes the sacrifice the way mothers are supposed to. Right?

BETH: [*off*] Emma!

EMMA: It's a fairytale. It's what he wrote. It's just not the kind of fairytale you read at bedtime though. Not the kind of fairytale anyone wants to hear.

BETH: [*off*] Emma! Where are you?

> EMMA *goes.*

> GRACE *is alone. She opens her journal and starts to write.*

> *And write,*

> *and write.*

SCENE SEVEN

EMMA *is finishing up getting ready for the award ceremony—putting on earrings, applying lipstick, that sort of thing.* GRACE *watches her.*

EMMA: Where the hell is she?

GRACE: I dunno.

EMMA: You called her?

GRACE: Twenty times.

EMMA: Why did you let her go off on her own?

GRACE: I didn't *let* her, she just did it.

EMMA: I thought you were looking after her.

GRACE: I was.

EMMA: And you let her wander off.

GRACE: She didn't wander off—she said she wanted to go for a walk.

EMMA: She never wants to go for a walk.

GRACE: Well, she did today.

EMMA: I'm going to be late.

GRACE: Just go—just go now.

EMMA: I can't go without her.

GRACE: Want me to call her again?

EMMA: She won't answer. She never answers. I don't even know why she has a phone.

GRACE: Sorry.

EMMA: Why didn't you go with her?

GRACE: She said she wanted to go on her own. Go for a walk to clear her head.

EMMA: What the hell was she thinking? She knows—she knows what time we have to leave. I told her. Did you tell her? Did you remind her?

GRACE: I didn't expect her to be out for so long.

EMMA: Fucking hell.

GRACE: Maybe she's lost.

EMMA: Oh god, don't say that.

GRACE: She'll be terrified.

EMMA: I know …

GRACE: Shit. This is my fault. I'm sorry. I messed up. I shouldn't have—

EMMA: Is this lipstick okay?

GRACE: Yeah.

EMMA: Not too much?

GRACE: No.

EMMA: I don't know …

GRACE: What if she's dead?

EMMA: She's not dead.

GRACE: She could have fallen in the canal.

EMMA: She's probably in a wine bar somewhere annoying the hell out of the staff—

GRACE: You're allowed to be worried.

EMMA: I'm not worried. I'm pissed off at her. I'm going to be so late.

GRACE: Just go.

EMMA: No, I don't want to go without her.

GRACE: Oh.

EMMA: She has to be there. I want her to be there.

GRACE: I hadn't … I didn't realise …

EMMA: What?

GRACE: That you actually want her there.

EMMA: Of course I do.

GRACE: Okay…

EMMA: I invited her didn't I?

GRACE: I thought Mum made you do it.

EMMA: No.

GRACE: Because they've gone away and someone had to look after her—

EMMA: I haven't spoken to Sophie.

GRACE: Oh. Right.

EMMA: I was always going to invite your nan.

GRACE: Okay.

EMMA: I'm only a writer because of her.

GRACE: Really?

EMMA: She was a beautiful writer.

GRACE: Was?

EMMA: She sort of … she lost it.

GRACE: Lost it?

EMMA: She got out of practice.

GRACE: But you can't just lose that sort of thing.

EMMA: I don't know.

GRACE: Have you?

EMMA: Have I what?

GRACE: Have you lost it?

EMMA: No. Yes. I don't know.

EMMA: Look at the time. I'm going to try her phone again.

GRACE: Don't bother. I'll go find her.

EMMA: I'll come with you.

GRACE: You'll be late.

EMMA: I'm going to be late either way. At least I can do something.

GRACE: It's a big deal. Tonight.

EMMA: According to Penny my whole future depends on it.

GRACE: Does it?

EMMA: There's important people there I need to impress.

GRACE: Um, you're getting this award—isn't that impressive enough?

EMMA: I hate this stuff.

GRACE: I'm proud of you.

EMMA: You're what?

GRACE: Proud.

EMMA: Oh.

GRACE: Sorry. That's weird—that sounds patronising or something—
doesn't it?

EMMA: No. Not weird. It's … nice. Thank you.

> *Beat.*

You still want to come?

GRACE: Um, I did, yes.

EMMA: Come then.

GRACE: What?

EMMA: Go get changed.

GRACE: Are you serious?

EMMA: I'll find her. You get ready.

GRACE: Are you sure?

EMMA: I wouldn't have said it—

GRACE: Oh my god. Okay. I'll, um, you'll be all right? Finding her?
On your own?

EMMA: You got something to wear?

GRACE: Yeah, I'll make do.

EMMA: Good.

GRACE: You're sure?

EMMA: I wouldn't have said it if I wasn't.

> GRACE *gathers up her bag and exits into the one of the rooms
> to change, as* EMMA *pulls on her coat and prepares to head
> outside.* EMMA *opens the door. And there is* BETH. *Just standing
> there. At the door.*

BETH: Couldn't find my key. Do I have a key?

EMMA: Where the hell have you been?

BETH: You're crying.

EMMA: No, I'm not.

BETH: I need the loo.

EMMA: Well, go on then, you know where it is.

BETH: Don't be so cross.

EMMA: We have to go, Mum.

BETH: What?

EMMA: The awards ceremony.

BETH: Yes, I know that, I know—

EMMA: You need to get ready.

BETH: I won't take long.

EMMA: Are you feeling alright?

BETH: I'm fine, I just wanted to walk.

EMMA: You don't walk.

BETH: I do.

EMMA: Well, walk, now, to your room and get dressed, please.

BETH: It's very pretty here.

EMMA: I know.

BETH: I had a martini.

EMMA: Did you?

BETH: It's all I drank in Paris.

EMMA: This isn't Paris.

BETH: I know that.

EMMA: Do you want help with your dress?

BETH: I'm not a child, Emma, I can still dress myself.

EMMA: Alright.

BETH: I resented it.

EMMA: I know.

BETH: And you.

EMMA: I know.

BETH: Did you?

EMMA: You've always been a very honest woman, Mum.

BETH: But I never regretted it.

EMMA: You didn't?

BETH: Not once.

EMMA: Me neither.

> *Pause*

BETH: That's good then. Isn't it?

EMMA: I don't know, Mum. I really don't know.

BETH: That story. The snow queen and the little boy with the glass lodged into his heart and his eyes.

EMMA: What about it?

BETH: I think I have that. A piece of that. Lodged here [*she taps her head*]—right there. And I can't … I can't seem to …

Pause

EMMA *pulls her mother in for a hug. It feels very unexpected. For them both. They stand in an embrace for a moment.*

EMMA: We really don't have a lot of time.

BETH: I know.

EMMA: The car will be picking us up—

GRACE *returns to the room—dressed for the ceremony, ready to go.*

GRACE: Nan! Oh my god. Nan!

BETH: You're all dressed up.

GRACE: I thought you'd drowned in the canal.

BETH: That's a little dramatic.

GRACE: You scared us.

BETH: I need to pee.

GRACE: Go, go, go.

BETH: [*exiting*] I am, I am, I am.

EMMA: And hurry up. We're late.

BETH: [*off*] We have plenty of time!

Pause

GRACE: You'll be great tonight.

EMMA: We'll see …

GRACE: [*indicating her outfit*] This okay?

EMMA: You look lovely.

GRACE: Oh, um, thanks? So do you.

EMMA: It will do.

GRACE: You want a drink or—

EMMA: Better not.

GRACE: No, no, of course.

Pause

Did you want to hear some of it?

EMMA: Of what?

GRACE: The book.

EMMA: I don't want to get into all that now, Grace—

But GRACE *has opened her laptop, and she starts to read.*

GRACE: Mum hadn't expected a visitor. I know because that's what she said when she heard a knock at the door. I wasn't expecting a visitor and her eyebrows buckled. She walked like she was in slow-motion, up the hallway to the door. And then she just stood there. Like she was scared or frozen or something. I wanted to see who this unexpected visitor was. I was imagining all sorts of crazy things because I was a kid then and that's what I used to do. Imagine things. I shouted *Open It* down the hall and Mum did.

She let out a little scream when she saw who her unexpected visitor was and for a second I thought I'd made her open the door to some sort of monster.

The unexpected visitor looked like a stretched-out version of Mum. She was taller and thinner, and her hair was much longer. Mum hugged her and she hugged Mum and they spoke very fast and quietly and suddenly she was rolling a suitcase down the hall right towards me.

Mum told her to sit, so she did and she winked at me from across the table. We were still eating dinner but the visitor didn't want anything, thank you but it looks amazing. I told her it was amazing and said the word the same way she did. Long and wavy. That's when Mum told me she was my aunty and, suddenly, I was in love.

BETH *enters.* GRACE *stops reading. They look at each other.*

BETH: Shouldn't we—

EMMA: Grace is reading her story.

GRACE: Oh no, it's okay, it's—

EMMA: Go on ..

GRACE: Um, but—

EMMA: Keep going …

GRACE: [*continuing to read*] Aunty was staying with us for a while because she needed a Little Rest. This Little Rest meant I had to be quiet and not run around the house like a tornado. A Little Rest pretty much sounded like the most boring thing in the world. Aunty said it was pretty much the most boring thing in the world but sometimes you need to be a little bit boring, now and then. Mum made this weird noise from her nose and walked away. Aunty said she had been far away, overseas and she tried to explain what that meant but I wasn't that little and I told her I knew what overseas was because we had been to Bali. Twice. She said I love Bali and I said I love Bali too and I copied the way she said love, in that long, wavy voice. That made her laugh and then Mum said let Aunty rest so I stopped talking. Aunty didn't. Aunty talked a lot. Mum gave her a cup of tea and she curled into the corner of the sofa like a skinny cat. She said it was good to be home and I wondered if she meant this, here, with us. Was this place her home? But I didn't ask her.

According to Dad this most definitely was not her home and some warning would have been nice and you can't just waltz in and out of people's lives like this. Dad didn't say this to Aunty. He said this to Mum with the door shut and the music on. I could still hear them. I think Aunty could too because she said let's go outside and we did.

Outside, Aunty looked at the stars. It was dark and I knew I should have been in bed. But I didn't tell her that. She pointed out stars and told me the pictures they made, when you joined them together like a dot-to-dot. I couldn't really see those things but I told her I could. Like one was an archer or something and another was a saucepan. I nodded when she said what they were and I looked up as high as I could and my neck hurt but I didn't care. I pointed to a bunch of stars and said they looked like a smile and she said I had a good imagination. But I already knew that. She gave me a hug and she smelled like the beach, like how I thought a mermaid would smell because, back then, I thought mermaids could actually be real things. We lay on the grass even though it was a little bit wet. Mermaids don't care about that sort of thing. I felt really small. Like the sky might just eat me up and no-one would notice. I told Aunty and she agreed. She always did that.

Mum shouted my name and I left Aunty outside, looking up at the stars.

Aunty slept on the couch and she was still there, fast asleep, the next morning. Her suitcase was open and it looked like all her clothes had tried to escape. They had spilled from the case and covered the floor. Mum shook her head and Dad went to work early.

I didn't want to go to school but Mum said that was non-negotiable and I said but Aunty will be lonely without us. I tried to say the word lonely the way Aunty would, all stretched out and curly. Mum didn't want to hear it and I had to go school end of discussion. She had forgotten to put her earrings on and her buttons were done up all wrong on her shirt but I didn't tell her.

That night I couldn't sleep because I could smell toast, which was weird because toast was always a morning smell. I had to know what was going on, so I silently slipped out of bed and headed towards the kitchen.

And there she was. Aunty. Making toast in the dark. In the dark. I knew I was supposed to be quiet but I laughed and she laughed too. She always did that. Laughed when I laughed. I waited for Dad to come out of his room and say what's going on but he didn't. She asked me if I wanted toast and I did because she did. I always did that. She used so much jam I couldn't see the toast and she didn't cut it into triangles or squares or anything. She just plopped it on the plate. Plop. Like that. We sat on the couch, which was also her bed, and ate. I asked her if she minded about the crumbs and she just shrugged like it was no big deal. I thought if Mum or Dad had seen us it would have been a very big deal, a huge deal, but I didn't tell her.

I didn't know what to say so I didn't say anything. Aunty didn't seem to mind. We just smiled at each other and made crumbs.

GRACE *stops reading, closes her laptop.*

GRACE: That's just the start of it, so … yeah …
EMMA: There's more?
GRACE: Yeah.
EMMA: We have time …
GRACE: We do?
EMMA: We do.

She sits down. GRACE *re-opens the manuscript and finds her place.*

THE END

RED STITCH | THE ACTORS' THEATRE

presents

Grace

1–27 FEBRUARY 2022

Playwright
Katy Warner

Director and Production Dramaturg
Sarah Goodes

Set and Costume Design
Jacob Battista & Sophie Woodward

Lighting Design
Harrie Hogan

Music Composition and Sound Design
Grace Ferguson

Lighting Mentor
Paul Jackson

Dramaturg & Assistant Director
Ella Caldwell

Dramaturg
Tom Healey

Stage Manager
Natasha Marich

Assistant Stage Manager
Holly Anderson

Emma – **Kate Cole**

Beth – **Jillian Murray**

Grace – **Mia Tuco**

This play was developed through Red Stitch's INK writing program.

RED STITCH | THE ACTORS' THEATRE

Artistic Director
Ella Caldwell

General Manager
Fiona Symonds

Production Manager
David Bowyer

Front-of-House Manager
Penelope Thomson

Development Manager
Patrick Fitzgerald

Marketing Partner
A Good Plan Group

RED STITCH ENSEMBLE

Ella Caldwell
Richard Cawthorne
Jung-Xuan Chan
Jessica Clarke
Kate Cole
Brett Cousins
Ngaire Dawn Fair
Daniel Frederikson
Emily Goddard
Kevin Hofbauer
Justin Hosking
Darcy Kent
Caroline Lee

George Lingard
Chanella Macri
Olga Makeeva
Dion Mills
Christina O'Neill
Joe Petruzzi
Dushan Philips
Tim Potter
Ben Prendergast
Kat Stewart
Sarah Sutherland
Andrea Swifte
David Whiteley

BOARD

Sophia Hall (Chair), Damon Healey (Treasurer), Henrietta Thomas (Secretary), Ella Caldwell, Catherine Cardinet, Humphrey Clegg, Andrew Domasevicius-Zilinskas, Belinda Locke, Michael Rich, and Sandra Willis.

We at Red Stitch acknowledge and pay our respects to Australia's First Peoples and Elders past and present, and offer our gratitude to the Boon Wurrung and Wurundjeri Woi Wurrung peoples of the Kulin Nation, on whose unceded lands we work.

THANK YOU

This development and production of *Grace* would not have been possible without the generous support of our donors and partners

KINDRED DONORS

Brian Goddard (in Memoriam)
The Lionel & Yvonne Spencer Trust
Maureen Wheeler AO & Tony Wheeler AO
Lyngala Foundation
Per & Ingrid Carlsen
Sieglind D'Arcy
Andrew Domasevicius & Aida Tuciute
Carrillo Gantner AC and Ziyin Gantner AC
John Haasz
The James Family Charitable Foundation
The Madeleine & Ed Neff Family Foundation
The Kate & Stephen Shelmerdine Family Foundation
Rosemary Walls
Anonymous
Beth Brown
Elise Callander
Caitlin English
Linda Herd
Graham & Judy Hubbard
Liz & Peter Jones
Michael Kingston
Alex Lewenberg
Jenny Schwarz
Christina Turner & Lyle Thomas
Jenny Veevers
Anita & Graham Anderson
Angela Benic and Peter Matkovic
Michael Brindley & Karinn Altman
Robin Carter

Julie & Ian Cattlin
Timothy Clark
Sophia Hall
Damon Healey
Edwina Mary Lampitt (in Memoriam)
The Lewis Langbroek Charitable Endowment
Barbara Long
Kate & Peter Marshall,
Kaylene O'Neil
Timothy Roman
Craig Smedley
James Syme,
Jane Thompson & Chris Coombs
Tony Ward & Gail Ryan
Ian & Grace Warner,
Graham Webster & Teri Snowdon
Margaret Yuill

MAJOR PARTNERS

Creative Victoria
City of Port Phillip
Cybec Foundation
Portland House
Lyngala Foundation
Malcolm Robertson Foundation
Playking Foundation
Copyright Australia Creative Development Fund

Rear 2 Chapel Street, St Kilda East, VIC 3183
http://redstitch.net/ | FB: @RedStitchTheatre | T: @redstitch
boxoffice@redstitch.net | 03 9533 8083

WRITER'S NOTE

This was not the play I had intended to write as part of the INK Program. In fact, I presented Ella and Red Stitch with a very different play all those years ago. But after our first conversation, Ella knew there was something else, something I was holding back on, and she encouraged me to write that play. This play. *Grace*.

What started as a play about sisters and a dying mother turned into three, very much alive, unapologetic women. Sisters. Mothers. Daughters.

That's all still there from that first play, in a way. But it grew into something more. A play about fairytales and stories, about memory and guilt, expectation and reality, and some big, gnawing questions about motherhood. What does it mean for a woman? To be a mother? Or not? To make that choice ... Or not ... I haven't found any answers. But I don't think I was looking for any.

I am so grateful to Ella and Red Stitch for the opportunity to write this work through the incredible INK Program. What an absolute privilege to have the time to really find something you want to write about and the support to write it. I am indebted to the women who have been in the workshop room across the various iterations of this work: Caroline Lee, Emily Goddard, Izabella Yena, Jillian Murray and Kate Cole, thank you for your time, talent, honesty and generosity. To Ella for pushing me to go further than I would have ever thought myself able. And, of course, Sarah Goodes for her skillful, thoughtful dramaturgy and beautiful direction. Since writing this play I now have a niece named Grace.

This play isn't named for her. This play isn't about her. But to all my nieces—Abby, Violet, Amelia, Billie, Tessa, Grace, Arielle—I love you and hope you will always have the courage to create, discover and tell your own stories. Because the stories you tell, the stories you share and the ones you keep are so important. As are you.

Katy Warner
Playwright

DIRECTOR'S NOTE

Ella approached me to direct a workshop and reading of Katy Warner's play *Grace* at the beginning of last year. Or was it the year before? Some time, somehow, during the slippery past year, in a brief opening we got together for a workshop and reading of this new work. Ella had organised the reading to take place at the Danish Club in the city. Seated on Danish chairs complete with sheepskin rugs draped over the backs, the audience enjoyed a traditional Danish meal of smoked fish and pumpernickel bread. While we made final tweeks to the script in an adjacent room we looked up to see a large, framed painting of Hans Christian Andersen quietly and patiently looking down on us. It felt fortuitous. Afterwards the audience stayed much longer than expected engaged in a fascinating and moving conversation about motherhood and how society treats women who choose not to have children or leave children. When the work was programmed, I was in.

For a long time, I have thought about why there are certain stories we rarely tell—women who choose to not have children or relinquish their roles as mothers are harshly judged and you are hard pressed to find many stories that touch on the subject. So I was captivated by Katy's play that touches so beautifully on the defensive armour that the character Emma has spun around herself to protect herself from judgment and how this has had such a huge impact on her life and relationships. During the design and rehearsal process we often spoke of the spiral-like feeling to the piece and about the cycles of motherhood and how it is common for a grandmother and granddaughter to enjoy an intimacy and warmth that has, for complex reasons, always eluded the grandmother and her own daughter. At times our society seems to project endless expectations around parenting— the bar always being set higher and higher on what children expect from parents and what parents expect of themselves and harsh judgment of others' parenting techniques and outcomes. The thing that struck me most about this piece was the idea that story can sometimes be enough. That the family dynamics Katy has captured through these beautiful characters demonstrate how we blame, exaggerate, lie, love, and annoy each other in attempts to get what we want and need but, most importantly, we tell each other stories—that stories are sometimes all we have to reach other each across seemingly impassable conflicts—that they are sometimes the only fragile vessel we have to navigate our way back towards each other.

This has been an extraordinary process steered so beautifully by Ella and Fiona and the wonderful INK program at Red Stitch. The time and resources allocated to this program are so important for new work. The actors Jillian Murray and Kate Cole were involved through most of the workshops, I think, and Katy has woven their voices into the piece beautifully. Both Jillian and Kate are actors I have wanted to work with for a long time and what they have brought to this piece is extraordinary. I directed newcomer Mia Tuco in her final year production at VCA in 2020 and have been looking for a production for us to work on together. The design team has been incredible: Jacob Battista and Sophie Woodward on set and costume and Grace Ferguson on composition and sound and Harrie Hogan on lights with Paul Jackson as mentor—you couldn't wish for a more dedicated and talented group of established and emerging artists. Thank you to Natasha Marich and Holly Anderson for their care and incredible attention to detail and lastly thank you to Katy Warner for trusting me with this beautiful play and for the incredible dialogue, complex nuanced characters and world you have created in this work *Grace*.

Sarah Goodes
Director

KATY WARNER
PLAYWRIGHT

Katy is a playwright and writer, living and working in Naarm (Melbourne). She studied at the Victorian College of the Arts, receiving a Master of Writing for Performance in 2012. Her plays have been presented across Australia, New Zealand and the UK. She is an AWGIE winner Best Children's Theatre for *Reasons to Stay Inside*; recipient of the Melbourne Fringe Award for Best Emerging Writer *These are the isolate*; and two-time nominee for a Green Room award for new writing *A Prudent Man and Spencer*. Her play, *nest*, was long-listed for Theatre503 Playwriting Awards (UK) and premiered at London's 2018 Vault Festival (Small Truth Theatre). Her plays have enjoyed national tours with Lab Kelpie and ArTour. Katy was a participant in the Besen Family Artist Program (Writer) at Malthouse Theatre and Melbourne Theatre Company's Women in Theatre Program. In 2018, she presented a new work, *K*, as part of the MTC Cybec Electric Readings season. Her fiction has received the Rachel Furnai Prize for Literature (Lip Magazine) and Overland Magazine's Neilma Sidney Short Story Prize. Her writing has been shortlisted for awards including the Lord Mayor's Creative Writing Prize and Grace Marion Wilson Emerging Writers Prize, and has been featured in Best Summer Stories (Black Inc.), The Slow Canoe and Overland. Katy's debut novel, *Everywhere Everything Everyone*, was published in 2019 by Hardie Grant and was shortlisted for the Readings Young Adult Book of the Year Award. She is currently working on her second YA novel, *Triple Threat*, to be published by Hardie Grant in 2022. Katy is a proud member of the Australian Writers' Guild.

SARAH GOODES
DIRECTOR & PRODUCTION DRAMATURG

For the past four years Sarah Goodes has been the Associate Artistic Director at Melbourne Theatre Company. Before this she was a Resident Director at the Sydney Theatre Company for four years. She is an award-winning theatre director recognised for bringing over 15 new Australian works to the mainstage. She has worked with many of Australia's leading actors including Helen Morse, Pamela Rabe, Sarah Pierse, Jacqueline McKenzie, Marta Dusseldorp, Mark Leonard Winter, John Gaden, William Zappa and Catherine McClements; and Australia's major theatre companies. She was Resident Director at Sydney Theatre Company from 2013 to 2016.

In 2018, Sarah won the Helpmann Award for Best Direction of a Play for her work on Lucy Kirkwood's *The Children* which opened at Melbourne Theatre Company and transferred to Sydney Theatre Company. Sarah directed the award-winning production of the world premiere of Joanna Murray Smith's *Switzerland* for Sydney Theatre Company, which toured to Melbourne Theatre Company. She received Best Director nominations for both the Helpmann and Sydney Theatre Awards for her work on *Switzerland*. Her production of *The Hanging* was nominated for Best Mainstage Production at the Sydney Theatre Awards. Sarah's production of *Golden Shield* for Melbourne Theatre Company received seven nominations at the 2020 Green Room Awards.

Other productions Sarah has directed for Melbourne Theatre Company include Laura Wade's *Home I'm Darling* starring Jane Turner, Louis Nowra's *Cosi* in a co-production with Sydney Theatre Company, the Helpmann Award nominated production of *JOHN* by Annie Baker; the Australian premiere of Lucas Hnath's *A Doll's House, Part 2* starring Marta Dusseldorp; and the world premiere productions of Anchuli Felicia King's *Golden Shield*, Stephen Sewell's *Arbus and*

West, Albert Beltz's *Astroman*, and Joanna Murray Smith's *Three Little Words*.

Sarah's productions for Sydney Theatre Company include: the Australian premiere of *The Children* by Lucy Kirkwood (with Melbourne Theatre Company); the world premiere of *The Hanging* by Angela Betzien; the Australian premiere of *Disgraced* by Ayad Aktar; *Orlando* by Sarah Ruhl starring Jacqueline McKenzie; *Battle of Waterloo* by Kylie Coolwell; the Australian premiere of *The Effect* by Lucy Prebble (with Queensland Theatre); the world premiere of *Switzerland* by Joanna Murray Smith; *Vere* by John Doyle (with South Australian Theatre Company); the world premiere of *The Splinter* by Hilary Bell; and *Edward Gant's Amazing Feats of Loneliness* by Anthony Neilson (with La Boite).

Other directing for theatre includes: for Belvoir, the world premiere of *The Sugar House* by Alana Valentine; *The Sweetest Thing* by Verity Laughton, *The Small Things* by Enda Walsh, *Black Milk* by Vassily Sigarev, *Elling* by Axel Hellsteius and *The Italian American Reconciliation* by John Patrick Shanley; for the Old Fitzroy Theatre, *The Schelling Point* by Ron Elisha, *Vertigo and the Virginia* by Sven Svenson, *Hilt* by Jane Bodie, *What Happened Was...* by Tom Noonan; for Darlinghurst Theatre, *The Unscrupulous Murderer Hasse Karlson Reveals The Gruesome Truth About The Woman Who Froze To Death On The Bridge* by Henning Mankell; for NIDA, *Scorched*; and for Sydney Opera House, *The Colour Of Panic* by Nicholas Hope.

Sarah is a graduate of both the University of NSW with majors in Literature and Theatre (final year at San Diego at UCSD where she performed with San Diego Rep) and the Victorian College of the Arts (University of Melbourne) in Directing. Sarah has taught and directed at the Australian Theatre for Young People and the National Institute of Dramatic Art.

JACOB BATTISTA
SET & COSTUME DESIGN

Jacob is a Melbourne-based theatre designer and practitioner. Jacob completed a Bachelor of Production at the VCA. Sophie and Jacob have recently co designed *Iphigenia in Splott* (Red Stitch) and *Burn This* (FortyFive Downstairs) in an exciting new collaboration. Some of Jacob's design credits include, *Hand to God, You're a Good Man Charlie Brown* and *Bad Jews* (Vass Theatre Group); *Rust and Bone* (La Mama); *True West* (Matchstick); *Songs for a New World* (Blue Saint); *MEMBER* (Fairly Lucid); *Frankie and Johnny in the Clair De Lune* (Collette Mann/45DS); *The Lonely Wolf* (Dirty Pretty Theatre/ MTC Neon); *Therese Raquin* (Dirty Pretty Theatre); *Carrie The Musical* (Ghost Light); *Love, Love, Love, Jumpers for Goalposts, Belleville* and *Out Of The Water* (Red Stitch). Jacob was the Associate Set Designer on *Shakespeare In Love* (MTC). Jacob was a recipient of a Besen Family Scholarship at the Malthouse in 2016 working with Marg Horwell on *Edward II* and is also a recipient of an Australia Council ArtStart Grant. Jacobbattista.com.au

SOPHIE WOODWARD
SET & COSTUME DESIGN

Sophie is a Melbourne-based Set and Costume Designer. Sophie graduated with a Bachelor of Production (Design) from VCA in 2010, winning the Beleura John Tallis Design Award in her final year. Sophie and Jacob have recently co-designed *Iphigenia in Splott* (Red Stitch Actors Theatre) and *Burn This* (FortyFive Downstairs) in an exciting new collaboration. Earlier design work from Sophie includes *Hungry Ghosts* (MTC), *The One* and *Mr Burns, A Post Electric Play* (FortyFive Downstairs); *Those Who Fall in Love like Anchors Dropped Upon the Ocean Floor, Between* the Clouds, *Pyjama Girl* and *Letters from the Border* (Hothouse Theatre); *Extinction, Rules for Living, You got Older, Uncle Vanya, The Honey Bees, The Village Bike, Wet House, Love Love Love, 4,000 Miles* and *Day One, A Hotel, Evening* (Red Stitch); *Thigh Gap, A Long Day's Dying, Conspiracy, Patient 12* and *The Savages of Wirramai* (LaMama); *Love Song* (Melbourne Fringe); and *The Sapphires, Glorious, Educating Rita, Shirley Valentine, Always Patsy Cline* and *All My Love* (Hit Productions). Sophie was Design Assistant on *An Ideal Husband* and *Twelfth Night* (MTC). You can view Sophie's work at **www.sophiewoodwarddesign.com**

HARRIE HOGAN
LIGHTING DESIGN

Harrie Hogan is a Naarm-based lighting designer. She began her training at Newtown High School of the Performing Arts before completing a bachelor's degree at the Victorian College of the Arts. Her recent design credits include *Kerosene* (Benjamin Nichol, 2021), *Very Nice Pot Plants* (Zachary Sheridan and Karla Livingstone-Pardy, 2021) *Analog* (Three Fates Theatre, 2021) and *Music of the Night* (Spears Entertainment, 2021). Harrie is a keen collaborator and proud to be counted amongst the growing number of women in her field.

GRACE FERGUSON
MUSIC COMPOSITION & SOUND DESIGN

Grace is a multi-instrumentalist, composer and piano educator based at Eastmint Studios in Naarm, Australia. Her works are a response to specific environments, finding a subconscious understanding and its culmination in sound; they often reflect curiosity in memory, intangibles and chance. Grace's practice encompasses a variety of music projects including the presentation of solo art music and ensemble collaborations, as well as composition and sound design for theatre, dance and film. Coalescing composed and improvised material, Grace's live performances draw from her classical training and other historic music traditions; although she often enjoys subverting many of these conventions through a modern, feminine lens.

PAUL JACKSON
LIGHTING MENTOR

Paul has designed lighting and/or sets and performance environments for most of Australia's leading performing arts companies and has lectured in design at the University of Melbourne, RMIT University and the Victorian College of the Arts. His work has featured in festivals and programmes in the United States, Asia, Europe and the United Kingdom. Paul was listed in *The Bulletin*'s Smart 100, was the Gilbert Spottiswood Churchill Fellow for 2007 and was an Artistic Associate at Malthouse Theatre from 2007-2013. He has received a Helpmann Award, seven Green Room Awards, two Sydney Theatre Awards, four Australian Production Design Guild Awards and a Critics' Award for Theatre in Scotland. Paul was awarded an Australia Council Fellowship (Theatre) for 2017-2019.

ELLA CALDWELL
DRAMATURG & ASSISTANT DIRECTOR

Ella is a theatre director, artistic director and actor. Growing up on the far south coast of NSW, Ella moved to Melbourne on a drama scholarship for her final years of school before studying Creative Arts at The University of Melbourne and auditioning for Red Stitch Actors' Theatre as a founding member in 2001. Elected artistic director in 2013, Ella has since launched Red Stitch's INK new writing program and created *PLAYlist*, a site-specific festival of new writing and music. Other highlights include the company's first international tour to Wuzhen Theatre Festival, building a touring partnership with Critical Stages and establishing the Kindred program.

Ella's recent directorial work includes the critically acclaimed Australian premiere seasons of *Oil* by Ella Hickson and *The Antipodes* by Annie Baker. In 2020 Ella directed her first audio play, *Watching* by Vidya Rajan and Morgan Rose. Previous directorial work includes the sold out season of Joanna Murray-Smith's *Fury* and Nick Payne's *Incognito*, both co-directed with Brett Cousins, and the world premiere of Caleb Lewis' *The Honeybees*. As an actor, Ella has performed in countless productions throughout theatres in Melbourne, most recently featuring in Morgan Rose's *desert, 6:29pm* at Red Stitch.

TOM HEALEY
DRAMATURG

Tom graduated from the Victorian College of the Arts in 1989. Over the past 30 years he has worked as a director, dramaturg and actor for theatre companies around the nation. His previous productions include: *American Song* (national tour), *Jumpers for Goalposts* and *The Shape of Things* (national tour, Red Stitch Actors' Theatre); *Heisenberg* (MTC); *The Kid* (Griffin); *The Spook* (Malthouse Theatre); *Elegy*, *The Sign of the Seahorse*, *Ancient Enmity*, *Insouciance*, *The Fat Boy* and *Falling Petals* (Playbox); *Let's Get it On* (Room 8); *Doris Day—So Much More Than the Girl Next Door* (Boldjack); *Disarming Rosetta* and *Inside Out* (Hothouse Theatre); *Good Evening* (Token) with Sean Micallef and Stephen Curry; *The Man In Black* (Folsom Prison Productions); Eddie Perfect's solo shows, *Drink Pepsi, Bitch!* (Malthouse Theatre and tour); and *Angry Eddie* (Chapel Off Chapel). Tom is currently the Associate Dramaturg at Red Stitch. Previous positions include Head of Acting and Directing at Flinders Drama Centre, Literary Manager at the Australian Script Centre, Artistic Director of the Australian National Playwrights' Conference and Artistic Associate at Playbox. He has been a proud member of the MEAA since 1989.

NATASHA MARICH
STAGE MANAGER

Following her bachelor studies in the visual arts (majoring in sculpture), Natasha pursued her growing interest in theatre-making and graduated from the production course at NIDA in the early 90s. Since then, she has sought to explore the creation of new works across a range of disciplines from puppetry and visual theatre to drama, comedy, music theatre, and contemporary dance, enabling her to work with many independent artists and companies and main-stage organisations alike. Working primarily as a touring stage manager she has been fortunate to have worked both nationally and internationally. Career highlights include the original touring production of Speaking in Tongues (by Andrew Bovell for Griffin and Playbox Theatres, 1997), Drink Pepsi, Bitch! (with Eddie Perfect, 2005-06), and The Pitch (with Peter Houghton for Critical Stages Touring, 2008) among many others. Recent stage management credits include Next Move for Chunky Moves (2018), Prague Fringe Festival (2019), Iphigenia in Splott for Red Stitch (2021), and Coral Browne: This F**king Lady with Amanda Muggleton, directed by Nadia Tass (2021, AKA Productions). The year 2021-2022 also marks Natasha's first foray as independent producer on Hearth Theatre's production of Arthur Miller's Death of a Salesman (showing in February at Forty-Five Downstairs). *Grace* marks a long association with Red Stitch since her introduction to the company as stage manager on *The Shape of Things* in 2005.

HOLLY ANDERSON
ASSISTANT STAGE MANAGER

Holly is a Stage and Production Manager working between Naarm/Melbourne and Meanji/Brisbane. Holly is a passionate creator with a love for new works, independent theatre and creating healthy collaborative work environments. Recent credits include: Stage Manager on the original Australian work *The Will to Be* (2019) dir. Mark Salvestro for Melbourne Fringe Festival, Assistant Stage Manager for *The Ghost Quartet* (2021) dir. Brandon Pape, Assistant Stage Manager/Assistant Production Manager for *Alternative Futures* (2021) dir. Kitan Petkovski, and Assistant Stage Manager on *Bluey's Big Play* (2021) regional tour.

KATE COLE
EMMA

Kate is a founding member of Red Stitch Actors Theatre, appearing in the one-woman play *Grounded* (Best Actress award in an Independent production 2015 Sydney Theatre Awards, Best Actress nomination 2014 Green Room Awards), *Incognito, Jumpers for Goalposts, Out of the Water, About Tommy, The Laramie Project 10 Years Later* (Arts Centre Melbourne) *Day One.A Hotel.Evening, Hellbent, Harvest* (Green Room Award Best Production) *The Pugilist Specialist, The Shape of Things, The Night Season, Push Up, Loyal Women, The Night Heron, Jesus Hopped the A Train, Where's My Money?, Pyschopathia Sexualis, Brilliant Traces, Unidentified Human Remains* and *Extremities*. Other theatre credits include *Circle Mirror Transformation, His Girl Friday* (both for Melbourne Theatre Company). In musical theatre, Kate has recently been in *Assassins* (Hayes Theatre Co, Sydney Opera House), *Ladies In Black* (QTC & MTC, National Tour), *Sweet Charity* (National Tour), *West Side Story* (Victorian State Opera,

IMG), *My Fair Lady* (VSO, IMG) and *42nd Street* (Her Majesty's Theatre, Sydney). Television credits include *The Doctor Blake Mysteries, 7 Types of Ambiguity, The Divorce, Final Sale, Borderline Murder* (both for US Lifetime Movie Network) NBC pilot *Frontier, Endurance Island, Dogwoman, Neighbours, Stingers, Crash Burn, Blue Heelers* and *Wentworth*. Kate trained in NYC and LA with Uta Hagen, and The Actors Studio lifetime members Marcia Haufrecht and Sharon Chatten.

JILLIAN MURRAY
BETH

Jillian has worked in Australia and in the U.K. She trained at East 15 Drama School (London) after completing studies at Monash University and Melbourne University. Theatre productions include: *The Blind Giant is Dancing, Garden of Granddaughters* (Sydney Theatre Company); *Travelling North* (The Lyric Theatre, London); *Moliere* by Bulgarkov, *Imaginary Invalid*; Anthill Theatre, Adelaide and Perth Festivals; *Lovesong* (Red Stitch); *De Stroyed*—a solo performance based on the writings of Simone De Beauvoir, three return seasons and a national tour of *L'Amante anglaise* by Marguerite Duras, *Magical Thinking* (Fortyfivedownstairs); *The Three Musketeers; Miss Julie, Lady in the Van* (Melbourne Theatre Company); *The Chairs* (Jenny Kemp, La Mama); *Away* (Neil Armfield); *Nice Girls; Good Time; Wolf; In Male Attire; World Made of Glass* (Playbox /Malthouse). TV productions include: *Jack Irish* (Series 1 & 2); *Stingers; Secret Life of Us; Embassy; Party Tricks; No Where to Hide; Skirts; Prisoner Festivals*. Film work: *Choir Girl; Body Melt; Spotswood; Georgia: Jenny Kissed Me*. Jillian received the Green Room Award in 2016 for Best Actor in an Independent Production (*L'Amante anglaise*) and has been nominated on three previous occasions. Later this year Jillian will tour nationally the solo work *The Year of Magical Thinking* by Joan Didion.

MIA TUCO
GRACE

Mia is a Melbourne-based actor, deviser and physical theatre performer who has worked and trained in Indonesia, Los Angeles, New Zealand and throughout Australia. She graduated from the Victorian College of the arts in 2020 with a Bachelor of Fine Arts in Acting. Her theatre credits at the VCA include *Earthquakes in London* (dir. Sarah Goodes), *Pool (no water)* (dir. Leticia Cáceres), *Mirror Mirror* (dir. Georgina Naidu), *Uncle Vanya* (dir. Budi Miller), *King John* (dir. Helen Trenos). Other recent theatre credits include *Theban Dolls* (dir. Saro Lusty Cavallari) and *Two Hearts* (dir. Katie Cawthorne). Mia is also an accomplished contemporary dancer and choreographer, performing in pieces by Jack Riley, Eliza Sanders and in 2018, Simone Forti's work *Huddle,* performed at the National Gallery of Victoria in partnership with MoMA. Mia's own choreographic work includes *informal get down* (2018) and *i was the angel in the poem you wrote* (2019).

RED STITCH ACTORS' THEATRE

Red Stitch is a creative hub, offering scope for artists to make work they are passionate about in a sector where such opportunities are limited. As the ensemble and executives of Red Stitch, we provide a platform where leading practitioners can hone their craft and take risks, and emerging artists can work alongside mid-career and seasoned professionals. We play a vital role in the development and presentation of new Australian works through our INK playwriting program, promoting local voices alongside acclaimed contemporary international work which may not otherwise be seen by local audiences.

www.redstitch.net

Red Stitch would like to thank the following supporters who generously contribute to our INK program.

CREATIVE VICTORIA

CITY OF PORT PHILLIP

Cybec Foundation

THE PORTLAND HOUSE FOUNDATION

Lyngala Foundation

MALCOLM ROBERTSON FOUNDATION

PLAYKING FOUNDATION

COPYRIGHT AGENCY CULTURAL FUND

Besen Family FOUNDATION

Kindred